WOODTURNING

with *Ray Key*

Bird's-eye maple bowl

WOODTURNING

with

Ray Key

B T BATSFORD LTD, LONDON

Dedication

To Liz and Darren

Acknowledgements

I would like to thank all my fellow woodturners in the UK and around the world, especially those I have had the pleasure of meeting; Tony Boase for his instinctive positioning for the best action shots, his wonderful object photography, plus his humour and friendship; my editors Abigail Glover and Emma Clegg who worked so hard on this publication; also all suppliers who provided tools and photographs – Axminster Power Tools Ltd, Craft Supplies UK Ltd, Craft Supplies USA Ltd, Graduate Lathe Co Ltd, Kel MacNaughton and Henry Taylor Tools Ltd – and woodturners who provided photographs of their own work: David Ellsworth, Bert Marsh, Dale Nish, Rude Osolnik and Bob Stocksdale.

Text and designs © Ray Key 1998

First published in 1998 by
B T Batsford Ltd
583 Fulham Road
London SW6 5BY

A catalogue record for this book is available from the British Library.

ISBN 0 7134 8149 8

Printed in Singapore

Photography by Tony Boase
Line illustrations by Robert Highton
Designed by DWN Ltd London

CONTENTS

INTRODUCTION

This is a major updating of the text that appeared in my first book, *Woodturning and Design*, which was published in 1985 in the UK and, as *Woodturning: A Designer's Notebook*, in 1987 in the USA. This revision of much of the information that was included in that book is presented in a much more practical style, which will, I hope, also prove to be more inspiring.

The years that have elapsed since the publication of *Woodturning and Design* have seen many changes in all aspects of life, including woodturning. There was a time when turning changed little and slowly, but over the past twenty years there have been some dramatic developments, and the last decade in particular has seen some especially significant steps forward. Tools, lathes, chucks, abrasives, finishes and techniques have changed, as have the videos, books and journals that relate to the craft.

Here and in the pages that follow I will give you an insight into how things have improved and give you informed options in many areas where woodturners are faced with difficult and sometimes confusing choices.

Just over a decade ago I was pretty pessimistic about the way in which woodturning was perceived by the public and the way it was handled within the education and training fields. These doubts have begun to fade, however, and recent developments have made me feel more optimistic.

The overall standard of work has been raised considerably, and educational establishments now seem to have a revived interest in the subject. The growth in interest in woodturning is, for the most part, hobby based, although there are many more turners earning a living from the craft than some twenty years ago. In addition, people with creative flair find that woodturning is one of the more accessible crafts. It is a creative hobby that can provide much enjoyment and satisfaction. In some cases the hobby develops into a new career, and many turners go on to sell some of the pieces they make at craft fairs; others are content simply to make things to give away to family and friends.

I suspect that stress is often one of the reasons for taking up woodturning. Despite all the benefits of modern living, there is no doubt that we have created a highly stressful way of living for ourselves. Is it any wonder that many people think nostalgically about the school woodwork shop and remember their first attempts at making a bowl or lamp base at the lathe?

It is encouraging to note that after a period of relative inactivity in woodturning during recent years, many schools are again purchasing lathes. Some schools have melded the new and the old disciplines in a very positive way. I recently taught at a school where computers were used to design and cost projects, and an informed choice of the most suitable material for the project was made. The youngsters I taught were aged from thirteen to sixteen, both girls and boys, and most took to turning like ducks to water, achieving some excellent results.

Another major step forward has been the formation throughout the world of national woodturning organizations and local clubs. Most meet on a regular basis, and the members share information and arrange demonstrations, lectures, discussions, competitions and visits to manufacturers or woodworking shows.

Then there is the worldwide phenomenon of seminars or symposia organized by the national bodies, which bring together some of the finest turners in the world who are willing to share and pass on their knowledge. These events inspire most of those who attend to set their sights higher, by showing the quality of work that can be achieved, and to raise their own standards of craftsmanship and design.

Most national bodies are now taking positive steps to encourage young people into the craft through such measures as seminars or training scholarships, reduced or free memberships, lathe loans and competitions. It is with the young that the future of woodturning lies, for at the moment something like 75 per cent of members of these organizations are over fifty-five years of age. This should and must change.

Unlike many other crafts, which have tended to

Masur birch hollow forms

receive more critical acclaim, establishment acceptance and credibility, woodturning has not been taught in colleges of art and design as a subject in its own right. This has certainly been to its detriment, but things are starting to change, albeit slowly.

All these developments have gradually led me to believe that the future of woodturning is brightening – at last, after some 3,000 years, it seems to be coming of age. Although it is not long since people who learned that I earned my living as a woodturner expressed a certain amount of disbelief, the general public's attitude seems to be undergoing a change, partly as a result of the increased number of turners throughout the world who are producing high quality work. Many of the leading woodturners create articles that are regarded as works of art, and when this happens, the craft as a whole becomes more respected. Collectors become involved, and museums and institutions begin to take an interest.

This recent recognition of the artistry that can be achieved by woodturners is not intended to suggest that the work produced by leading turners in the past was any less worthy. For the most part, however, the turner used only to produce components of larger pieces and objects for use of some kind – from a chair's stretcher rail to a balustrade, from a child's spinning top to a drinking vessel.

When you look at the turned works made many centuries ago and housed in a number of museums, it is evident that the turners then were no less accomplished than the craftsmen working with other materials. That the turner was not regarded with the same high esteem may simply have been because even when at his most creative, the object was viewed as functional and, therefore, humble. Or it may have been because the making process was considered less mysterious or even that the material itself was thought to have little value, as trees were cut down for firewood or used for construction purposes.

Wood should, in fact, be treated with reverence. It is one of the most versatile materials in the world and one of our few renewable resources, a message that is, thankfully, at last being understood.

EARNING A LIVING

Earning a living from any craft is always difficult, and for many the financial rewards will never be high. Nevertheless, the satisfaction of making some sort of livelihood from the creative use of your hands can be reward enough.

Before you embark on any career in the crafts there are many things to consider. In order to succeed, you must be much more than a fine craftsman. It will help if you have developed a sound understanding of the material you use. You will never stop learning how to recognize and use to

best effect any natural beauty that lies within a piece of wood, but you need to be at least some way along the road. You need, too, to be able to produce in a proficient and economic way a range of work that is identifiably your own. Then you have to sell your work, and a pleasant, outgoing, friendly attitude will help.

So you are a maker, a designer and a salesman so far, but it doesn't stop there. You must also become a businessman, an accountant and professional in all your business dealings. Most importantly, you must set yourself realistic, but high, standards and objectives. Good health and whole-hearted support from your partner are also invaluable, as there may be disappointments along the way. Without the belief and encouragement of my wife, Liz, I might well have stopped being a woodturner some years ago.

Once you have mastered the art of woodturning you can use your skills in a number of ways – making reproduction furniture, restoring antique pieces, in architecture, chair making, producing components for furniture and parts for toys and games, and making both functional and decorative items for the home. Many turners combine a number of these areas and may embrace them all at some time or another. I concentrate on designing and making domestic pieces and one-off decorative objects, but at one time I did a lot of work for interior designers and furniture makers, as well as for a giftware manufacturer.

When I first started earning my living from woodturning, I offered a range of twenty-three different domestic items, many in different sizes, giving a choice of seventy items, not including design options! I was naive to think that a

Burr elm bowl

range that big was practical for a one-man business to produce on a wholesale basis. Time was to prove this impracticable. The need to carry a large timber size range inventory, plus a lot of accessories, tied up far too much money. Some orders received requested just one of a certain item. To produce one of a production item for the most part is impractical and unprofitable. This type of work needs to be produced in reasonable quantities – permitting small-scale batch production – to allow you to work speedily and economically. If you are retailing direct to the public, you can produce a larger product range because you do not have to offer set sizes and can often use up offcuts. You can also ask a higher price than if you are wholesaling the articles you make. Over the years, I have rationalized my domestic wholesale list down to just three different products – salad bowls, platters and chopping boards, which are offered in a range of sizes. This adds up to a more manageable list of nineteen items. You might think this would be rather boring and repetitive and you would be right if that was all I produced, but since 1976 I have also been making one-off gallery items.

Today I think of myself principally as a headstock turner, a maker of bowls, platters, dishes, vessels and boxes, but within each area I always aim to apply a wide design spectrum. Bowls, for instance, range from small pieces of porcelain-like delicacy, to large, rugged and sculptural items.

MARKETING

What you make and how you market it are, of course, interlinked, but if your work is similar to mine here are a few thoughts. I have always sold 80 to 90 per cent of what I make on a wholesale basis through shops, including galleries, craft and kitchenware shops, that purchase direct rather than on sale or return. My sales to the public have come through our shop (which we ran between 1971 and 1984), through my local county designer–craft guild, through two or three top quality craft shows and through overseas seminars and teaching assignments.

You might want to consider direct sales from a workshop/showroom, through craft fairs or through agricultural shows. Many craftsmen like to attend shows because of their market atmosphere and the opportunities they offer for contact with fellow craftsmen and the public. There is also the advantage that you obtain your full retail price by selling direct to the public. Shows are also a great opportunity to meet customers who may be interested in commissioning work in the future. However, do bear in mind that the cost of your stand, of accommodation and of travel and the loss of time out of your workshop must be deducted from your profits.

Many galleries operate on a sale or return basis, an arrangement I have always tried to resist, although I have given a little ground in recent years to a selected few. If, for example, they have purchased a number of best-selling pieces, I am prepared to let them have a few higher priced items on sale or return.

EXHIBITIONS

I have always enjoyed exhibitions. They present a challenge that usually brings out the best in me, both in work quality and concept. My feeling is that any exhibition should feature a selection of the work for which one is best known, but that there should also be plenty of inspiring new work.

To date my work has been shown in over 150 exhibitions worldwide, from the UK and the USA to South America and South-east Asia.

I have a strong perfectionist streak, and this drives me constantly to seek to improve the things I create. Even so, there is much around that I would like to deny having made! I generally take the view that any piece is a stepping-stone along the way to doing things better. If you possess a similar force, it is important to control it, or you may become too self-critical, which will slow you down and lead to frustration.

Macassar ebony vessel

INFLUENCES AND INSPIRATION

When I was nine, a perceptive teacher told my mother that I would never be an academic but would always earn a living with my hands, and so it has proved. There can be no doubt that from our first days we are influenced by the things and the people around us. My father, who was always making things, encouraged me to work with my hands, and my rural upbringing gave me a love of natural materials. Even then, wood was the material that attracted me, and I spent hours fretworking and carving in a small shed equipped with a workbench.

My first recollection of seeing anyone turn wood was at a flower show in Leamington Spa, Warwickshire. The turner was Charlie Gardener, who came from Warwickshire. A tremendous character, he was invited to exhibit at the Royal Agricultural Show and the Chelsea Flower Shows.

In my early teens, the school woodwork shop held a special fascination, and my first experience of woodturning was in 1956, when I created a wooden handle for a small garden fork made in the metalwork department. In fact, I had no feeling for metal, much preferring the warmth of wood, and I knew that wood was the material with which I wanted to earn my living.

On leaving school, I started a five-year pattern-maker apprenticeship, during which I learned to read complicated engineering drawings and make objects to fine limits, plus casting and production methods. Perhaps most significantly I did a lot of turning as most of the men there hated this aspect of the job. I then moved on to work with fibreglass, a dreadful material for any self-respecting woodworker to deal with. Finally I spent eight years as a clay modeller in the UK Chrysler styling studios, which gave me an insight into design, prior to making the leap into being a full-time woodturner.

In 1965 I bought my first lathe, an Arundel ER5. That year proved to be one of the most significant in my life, for I met my wife, Liz, the greatest single influence on my life and a wonderful moral support in many things I have done since.

Most evenings found me in the workshop, working on the lathe, with Frank Pain's *The Practical Woodturner* propped up in front of me as I tried to learn the techniques needed to become competent. The pleasure of turning wood is heightened when you have learned to manipulate the tools correctly, enabling you to cut the forms you have in mind cleanly. I read articles by Geoff Peters and Peter Child and made many of the projects suggested at a time when the craft revival was gathering momentum, and I spent weekends and holidays visiting craft shops and craftsmen, searching for turners of quality.

Among those who impressed me most were George Sneed, whose simple, pure forms were ahead of public taste at the time, and John Trippas and Dennis French, who produced domestic pieces. It was not necessarily the objects they produced, but the sheer consistency of their standards that impressed me. I spent long hours practising, and my technique and design skills gradually improved as I aimed for the standards set by the craftsmen whose work I admired.

A range of turned objects made in 1977 following traditional design principles

A similar range of objects also made in 1977 in a more contemporary and personal style

An exhibition of my work was arranged in a Warwick bookshop in 1971, and, encouraged by its modest success, Liz opened a small craft shop later that year to sell my work and other craft-related products. By 1st July 1973 we had decided that I would try to make a full-time living from woodturning. We moved to Evesham, Worcestershire, and opened a small craft shop. For the first three years the income from the shop was greater than I was able to generate as a turner as I strove to establish myself, but from then on turning produced more income than the shop ever did, and in 1984 we finally closed it.

I continued to learn. David Pye's wonderful boxes caught my eye, as did the work of the Raffan brothers. In 1976 Peter Dingley, the owner of a well-known gallery in Stratford-upon-Avon, encouraged me to use a wider range of timbers and to produce work of a more decorative and aesthetically pleasing nature than the functional items on which I had been focusing. A visit to the Oxford Gallery that year led the formidable Joan Crossley-Holland to comment: 'You should be on the Crafts Council Index!' Fuelled by this encouragement from someone so well regarded in the craft world, I applied to the Crafts Council in 1977. I was asked to submit five pieces of work, and to my delight the selection committee was kind enough to put me on the Index. This stamp of approval opened many doors, and I started to receive exhibition invitations frequently. My first major exhibition was in late 1977, at Collection Gallery in Birmingham. I made some eighty items in twenty different timbers especially for the occasion, and these were well received. I have since taken part in numerous gallery exhibitions worldwide.

In 1979 I met Bob Stocksdale from the USA at a James Krenov Seminar at Parnham House – the influence that this John Makepeace institution has had on the entire

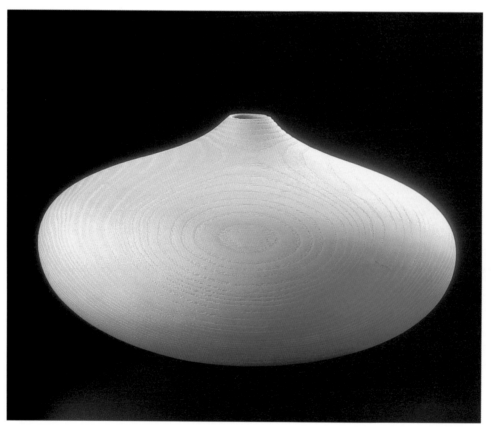

Lunar pot in white ash by David Ellsworth

woodworking world is unquantifiable. My meeting with Bob, who is, perhaps, the best known bowl turner in the world, made a great impression on me. His very thin and delicate bowls made full use of the wood's natural beauty, and he created wonderful aesthetic forms normally associated with fine porcelain. His influence led to my bowls becoming much lighter and finer. The first International Woodturning Seminar was held in the UK in 1980, and it proved to be a great stimulus to all who attended. Bob Stocksdale was one of the overseas presenters, along with David Ellsworth and Stephen Hogbin. Their presentations stimulated and awakened most of us into looking at wood in a different way. Possibilities most of us had never thought of emerged, and we all left the seminar questioning our own work. This was the first major event at which I, too, had been a presenter, and it was something I greatly enjoyed. Being able to share ideas with other turners and learning from

them is immensely satisfying. It was tempting to launch headlong in their direction, but I was aware that the UK market is much more conservative than the USA. New ideas are often slow to catch on, and timing is critical.

In 1981 the 10th Woodturning Symposium, organized by Al Le Coff, was held in Philadelphia, USA. The presenters included Ellsworth, Hogbin, Moulthrop, Stirt, Stocksdale, Gilson, Mitchell, Stubbs, Linquist, Osolnik, Doyle and Nish – a list that reads like a *Who's Who* of creative woodturning. Once our interest was registered, Richard Raffan and I were added to the list. This event was to prove one of the most significant happenings in both our careers, and opportunities we had not dreamed of came our way – seminars, publishing, teaching, demonstrating, USA gallery sales – as a result of our attendance.

At the symposium, Richard and I had our first face-to-face meeting with Dale Nish, who had already asked us to

Exotic bowls by in African blackwood and Lignum vitae by Bob Stocksdale

feature in his book, *Master Woodturners*, an invitation we were delighted to accept. Dale has been a source of inspiration for countless woodturners all over the world, but for no one more than me. We have met almost every year since, and he has been the source of many invitations to seminars and workshops. In more recent years, the funding for and making of my three box-making videos came about with his support. He even directed them. The

making and marketing by Henry Taylor's of a range of woodturning tools, developed by me over the years, stemmed once again from a Dale Nish suggestion.

The 1981 symposium was accompanied by the Turned Object Show, featuring about a hundred exhibits all with the overriding theme of innovation and excellence. After the symposium, I stayed with David Ellsworth, which proved to be a tremendous experience. A group of us worked and experimented in the workshop. This visit was inspirational, practical and yet unsettling. The practical aspect came with the developments in power-sanding methods that are now being used by turners worldwide. The unsettling aspect for me was that it seemed possible to earn a living from

Turned wooden candlesticks in macassar ebony showing a fine understanding of balance and proportion by Rude Osolnik

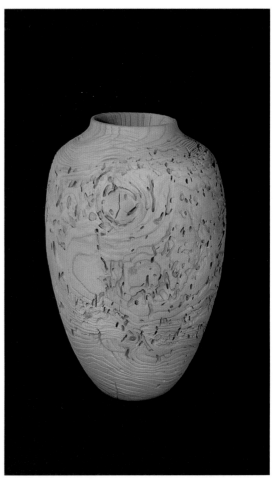

Wormy ash vessel by Dale Nish

Spalted elm vase by Bert Marsh

turning by making 'one-offs' or 'one-of-a-kind objects' in the USA. This idea greatly appealed to me, and on my return I decided the utilitarian work had to go. The result was a lack of sales and orders, fuelled by the recession at that time, which almost ruined us. Realizing that my timing was wrong, I returned to reality just in time and fortunately was commissioned by a leading kitchen shop to produce salad bowls. I still supply them and have never felt confident enough since those hard times to tread that road again.

It has been my pleasure over the years to have been invited to present seminars and run workshops in the USA, Canada, New Zealand, Ireland, Germany, Norway and France. Any influence or inspiration that I may in some small way have been able to impart has been more than reciprocated. I have mentioned the names of just a few people who have made a great impression on me, but there are countless others whom I respect, not just for their work but for their contribution to the

woodturning movement. I consider myself fortunate to count many of them as good friends. Among them are Del Stubbs, for his unique touch and boyish enthusiasm; Giles Gilson, for his creative imagination; Hans Wiessflog, for his craftsmanship and design; and David Ellsworth for his pioneering spirit and skill. I also admire Ed Moulthrop, for the sheer scale of his work; Rude Osolnik, for his sixty-year contribution of innovation, quality, teaching and for his love of wood and turning; and Johannes Rieber, the most complete woodturner I know. Last but by no means least, I must add Bert Marsh, for many reasons, not least his friendship, the quiet quality of pureness in his work, his pursuit of excellence and his belief that you should create time, occasionally, to make things just for yourself. Some of the aforementioned are the warmest, most enthusiastic and inspiring human beings it has been my pleasure to meet.

EQUIPMENT, TIMBER AND TECHNIQUES

This section reflects the tremendous changes that have come about in the world of woodturning in the past ten to fifteen yeas. Lathes, tools and chucks have, for the most part, all improved in quality. Choice is greater now than ever, and many hobby turners are confused by similarities of much of what is available. I shall do my best to explain the differences.

A wider range of timber has also become available to the hobby turner through specialist outlets.

Finally, techniques continue to evolve to cope with the steady flow of new tools that come on to the market at regular intervals.

Key specialist tools (see page 29)

EQUIPMENT

As with most crafts, there is a wide range of equipment available and it is possible to buy the minimum amount economically or to spend a small fortune on acquiring the latest tools and machinery. Outlined below are some pieces of equipment you will need to invest in, starting with the lathe.

LATHES

It is best if you are able to identify where your greatest interest lies before you buy a lathe, but most people I know want to try and work in both fields – that is, spindle and headstock turnery – although in time they tend to favour one area of work over the other. Many turners later regret buying their first lathe because it soon limits their development. You must choose carefully because it will be your single biggest investment.

There can be no doubt that most lathes represent a compromise in engineering terms, largely because of costs. Many of the less expensive machines try to provide everything but finish up offering nothing successfully. Some lathes can be used for either spindle or headstock turning, and these are built with fewer compromises, and some of the models at the top end of the market have eliminated almost all compromises.

There have been a number of significant developments in lathe design in recent years, and some features that were in only limited use have become common. These features are twin, round, steel bed bars (ways in the USA), pivoting headstocks and variable speed. Perhaps the greatest

advance has come recently in the form of fixed-head lathes, which allow you to turn outboard in a right-handed manner.

Following is a brief overview of the lathe market, outlining some of the many choices, from those starting at £200 through to those that will cost £6,500. Most, however, are in the £500 to £3,000 price range.

Twin round bed bars

This system of solid steel bed bars, often chromed, has been adopted by a number of manufacturers. Most are bench-mounted machines, and the diameter of the bars increases as the models get bigger. These machines seem to enjoy varying degrees of success when it comes to rigidity and the locking of the cross-slide tool rest holder (banjo). Some do not lock well, and the last thing you need is your cross-slide to move while you are turning. Models with a flat top to the bars, or some form of saddle that increases the metal-to-metal surface-locking area, will be better than those that rely on just the flat section of the cross-slide making contact on the round bar. A good cam-locking lever method will also help. I am still old-fashioned enough to believe flat-topped horizontal bars, preferably in cast iron, still provide the best solution.

Pivoting headstocks

Pivoting headstocks were increasingly popular in the early to mid-1970s and are now commonplace. A number of bigger capacity machines are being built. They are especially popular with people who have only a limited working area because it is possible to turn larger diameters in a right-handed manner. They also overcome much of the tendency of the bed bars getting in the way of the much longer-handled tools required in faceplate work. These lathes can never be as solid as those with heads that do not pivot, but several have some excellent features. I find that their major strength lies when they are used in the spindle-turning mode. If your preference is for faceplate turning, there are better options.

Right-handed outboard turning

In the past, the greatest strength of standard lathes was for spindle turning. Headstock turning was a compromise for most. You had to turn outboard in a left-handed manner, and as the majority of people are naturally right handed, this was a less natural and efficient way of working (although you do need to become ambidextrous in turning to be truly efficient). To overcome this problem, most professional turners had at least two lathes – one dedicated and built especially to allow for right-handed headstock work (a short bed), and another for spindle work. However, a major development in recent years means that this is no longer necessary. The spindle thread is now the same on both sides of the lathe, which makes it possible for the same chucks and faceplates or any compatible threaded device to be used on either side.

So that this can happen, the motor has to be reversed, a process that is made possible and safe by electronic interlocking switches. On and off switches are fitted either side of the headstock, and various safety devices are built in. The credit for this development in Britain goes to Gabor Lacko, an electronics engineer, and a number of manufacturers now use this system worldwide.

Variable speed

Variable speed has been around for years, but many systems left a great deal to be desired. Some relied – and indeed still rely – on split pulleys, which are usually noisy and heavy on belt wear, or on one pulley size on shaft and motor, which is unsuccessful because of loss of torque. With new-generation electronics, inverters, three-phase motors and the retained use of stepped pulleys, there is no loss of torque. Speeds can be set much lower or higher, are infinitely variable and very quiet. I converted to this system

as recently as 1995, because I had previously been worried about the shortcomings mentioned earlier. Once you have this new system, you will wonder how you managed before. There are a number of lathes available that, although embracing the new technology, are underpowered. Any lathe fitted with less than a 1hp (0.75kW) motor should be thought of as being useful for small work only.

I have two variable speed lathes, each fitted with 1.5hp (1.1kW) three-phase motors that run on a single-phase supply.

Mini-lathes

These machines are ideal for those who want to make small items like lace bobbins, light pulls, bottle stoppers and spinning tops. They are usually only about 18in (460mm) long, so space is not a problem. The most popular and commonest of these machines are the Klein, Carba-Tec, Little Gem and Vicmarc.

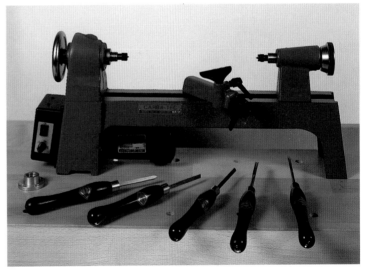

Carba-Tec mini-lathe

Bench-mounted lathes

These come in various shapes, sizes and capacities, with pivoting heads and fixed heads, various stepped pulley combinations, some with variable speed, and in a tremendous price range. Any machine of this type needs to be mounted on a very solid base to damp down vibration, but many are being supplied on lightweight bent metal legs that are wholly unsuitable. Names like Coronet (now no longer produced), Record, Tyme, Delta and Nova are synonymous with the smaller capacity lathes of this type. Larger versions, like Myford, Poolewood and Apollo, are the smoothest running.

Cast fixed-head lathes

There are a number of models to choose from, that either have the bed and headstock unit cast in one piece or with the castings assembled and then mounted on a prefabricated metal understructure. The best known of

Cast fixed-head lathe by Woodlathe

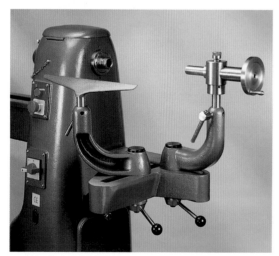

Graduate one piece casting fixed-head lathe

these are Woodfast from Australia and the General from Canada, both of which are well-proven lathes. I have worked on both kinds and each has some good features, including excellent swing capacity over the bed. A newcomer to this field using both cast and welded construction in a revolutionary concept is the Oneway from Canada. This is a large capacity lathe that has made quite an impression in a short time with serious turners.

The heaviest, and in my view the best, lathes have the complete headstock pedestal cast in one piece, with the cast beds bolted on to this. The top of the range in this group is the British-made Graduate, which thanks to Richard and Ted Henning and Gabor Lacko has been brought up to date. Now the swing capacity over the bed has increased it is top of the pile again.

CHUCKS AND CENTRES

Over the years, there have been significant developments in the way we mount and hold wood in the lathe, but many of the methods that have been used for centuries are still valid today. The days of green baize, cork, labels and so on to cover up the tell-tale faceplate screw holes should be a thing of the past.

Headstock turning

Mounting a block of wood for this type of turning has usually been by way of faceplates and screw chucks. A number of developments have improved these long-established methods, while others offer other options for holding work.

Faceplates

Faceplates are available in a very wide range of sizes, and have traditionally been used for mounting anything to be made from cross-grained wood. Direct, three-screw fixing through the plate into the block of wood to be turned is the most common method, with a penetration of screw of $\frac{1}{2}$–$\frac{3}{4}$in (12–18mm). As common sense would suggest, more screws and with greater depth penetration are needed for large, heavy blocks. Larger end-grained work is also often mounted in this way, but the screw penetration into end grain needs to be much greater as it does not hold as well.

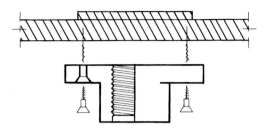

Fig 1 Wooden friction chuck

Attaching a waste block to a faceplate offers a number of alternative fixings – by way of tenon/spigot friction fit or any number of glued joints, such as contact adhesive, hot melt, PVA white/yellow, cyano-acrylate (Superglue), newspaper/glue joint and so on. Direct fixing of double-sided tape to the faceplate and base of the item to be turned is also a possibility for thin section work. All these methods will suffice, but a less aggressive approach with the tools is required, as a dig in with the tool can cause the work to fly from the lathe.

Faceplate rings

I like to use faceplate rings a great deal in batch production, mostly for bowls and dishes. I have twenty of them, made of die-cast aluminium, and they are at most a quarter of the price of an equivalent sized faceplate. They are used in conjunction with an expanding dovetail chuck, which allows work to be mounted on and removed from the lathe very quickly. They are excellent in a production workshop or in the classroom.

Screw chucks

The introduction of parallel-machined screws has made the use of the old tapered wood screw almost a thing of the past. The wood holding is so much firmer on good parallel screws, which are made from stainless steel and have a knife-edge thread, which cuts the wood fibres. Poor screws have a flat on the top of the thread, which crushes, rather than cuts the fibres. The good screws allow you to remove and remount work accurately every time. The one thing you need to remember is to drill a compatible pilot hole for the size of screw being used – that is, a ⅜in (9mm) parallel screw needs a ¼in (6mm) pilot hole. The old tapered ones would pull on to a smaller pilot hole, but hold the work only half as well.

Pin chucks

Pin chucks are extremely useful for producing a wide range of goods, from bowls, particularly natural-topped ones, to pepper mills. The original pin chuck, which is still widely used, is a parallel shaft of metal, in various diameters – ¾in (18mm) up to 2in (50mm) is common. It has a machined flat on it and is mounted into another chuck body. The work to be turned has a hole drilled into it, compatible with the pin size to be used, and a loose pin is placed on the flat. This rolls and locks the work to be turned under the thrust of the lathe's inertia. There can be problems with this system, however. For example, when it is used with wet wood, the fibres often swell and great difficulty can be experienced when you try to remove the work from the lathe. Alternatively, in softer woods the hole can become enlarged, which leads to the work spinning, making tooling difficult.

Faceplate (1), faceplate ring (2) and screw chucks (3 and 4)

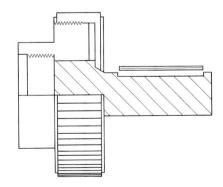

Fig 2 Pin chuck

The development of the four-way segment split pin for scroll chucks eliminates both of these problems.

Cup or bell chucks

The cup or bell chuck, used for holding end-grained wood, is an old favourite with many turners, although it is one I seldom use. The item to be held normally has a slightly tapered tenon/spigot turned on it, which is then driven into the cup or bell with a mallet for friction holding.

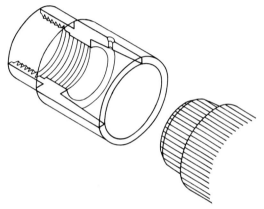

Fig 3 Cup chuck

Multi-Purpose Chucks

This is the area where the greatest development has taken place in recent years. The chucks whose praises I sang back in 1984, although still being made and working just as well, have been superseded twice since then.

There are three major types of chuck, and, in the main, they all do similar things although in different ways. Most have four jaws that expand and contract. They grip the work, either externally or internally, with tapered dovetail undercut jaws.

There are a great number of variations of these chucks in a wide range of sizes. With some models, the complete set of jaws is removed and another size inserted; alternatively, the jaws are exchanged and bolted on to a master set in some way or another.

Cone spread and contraction chucks

These are the first-generation multipurpose chucks. The jaws normally expand under compression. As the chuck body's outer ring is tightened down, a tapered cone centre spreads the jaws. Contraction is obtained by the removal of the cone and the insertion of a totally different type of jaw. Other systems contract and expand the same jaws, through the insertion or removal of ring cones. All chucks of this style rely on two levers to lock the jaws firm, and there is a wide range of jaws and accessories available. Most are of a modest price, and as a result, these chucks still find favour with those on a tight budget or who turn only occasionally.

Cone spread and contraction chuck

Two-lever scroll chucks

These are the second-generation multipurpose chucks, and they mostly offer a wider range of options than the cone type and are more consistently accurate in use. The principal of the scroll mechanism, which has always been used in engineering chucks, has been adapted for woodturners only in recent years. The scroll affords a two-way gripping action, with one set of jaws, which are internal through expansion and external through contraction. The jaws are, of course, of a different size. There is much greater lateral movement of the jaws than on the cone type, and the accuracy of the tenon/spigot or inset dovetail needed to grip your work is not as crucial. All sorts of alternative jaws, in a wide range of sizes, are either bolted on to a master set or exchanged completely. They are contracted and expanded to grip the work by the use of two levers that are either C-spanners or tommy bars. These requirements mean that both the cone and this type of scroll chuck take time to operate and can lead to frustration, especially if you make your living from turning. There is a feeling that a certain amount of brute force is required to secure the work safely, and three hands would be better than two. The lathe spindle is best locked.

One-key scroll chucks

There are two sorts available at present. One kind uses a toothed key, similar to a drill chuck, with matched teeth on the chuck body. The other is a self-centring four-jaw engineer's chuck with a square key, adapted for woodturners – this is the ultimate model, in my opinion, and I use it to produce up to 80 per cent of my work. They are the fastest-acting, the most versatile, best-gripping and strongest chucks, but are, of course, more expensive.

No brute force is required to secure or release the work. It is held in one hand, while a firm turn of the key with the other hand is all that is required to secure blocks of wood. A wide range of jaws allows you to hold almost anything you want on the lathe.

One-key scroll chuck

Spindle turning centres and chucks

There has been a number of developments in spindle-holding methods although not quite so many as in headstock turning. Almost all drive centres and small chucks for spindle turning have a morse-taper shaft, which fits into a compatible one in the hollow headstock or tailstock of the lathe. They are normally 1MT and 2MT, although some are 3MT.

Headstock end

Two- and four-prong are the most common drive centres for general work. These are available in a wide range of diameters and prong lengths. A recent development has been the Stebcentre, which has a serrated drive ring and a spring-loaded centre point. This enables work to be mounted and removed safely without switching off the lathe.

There are square drive centres for lace bobbin making or any other articles that are made from very small squares. Mandrels are made for making light pulls, pens and many other products.

Tailstock end

Dead cone or ring centres have traditionally been supplied with lathes, but I think they are a thing of the past. The future lies with revolving, but buy a good one. Many have removable tips that give the option to use cone or ring, often in different sizes, and a flat-ended tip for non-marking pressure support is found with some.

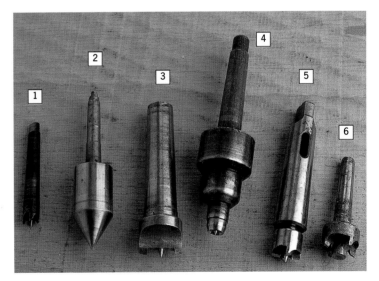

Small four-prong drive centre (1), revolving cone centre (2), large two-prong drive centre (3), revolving ring centre (4), four-prong drive centre (5) and four-prong lamp drive centre (6)

Conical friction chuck

This is a useful piece of equipment for those who want or need to produce split turning work. Small patterns, reproduction work and antique restoration often call for this process. You insert a chuck in both the head- and tailstock ends of the lathe.

Jacob's chuck

Usually mounted on a morse-taper shaft, this kind of chuck is extremely useful. It is used mainly for drilling in the lathe, either rotating in the headstock end or used stationary in the tailstock. It can also be used to hold small items of turnery by gripping on a small turned spigot. This chuck is pretty well essential if you do not have a pillar drill but produce items that need drilling.

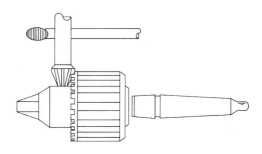

Fig 4 Jacob's chuck

TURNING TOOLS

There are three main types of turning tool – gouges, chisels and scrapers – and there is a wide range of variations of each type. Nearly all are made from high-speed steel (HSS), and they hold their edge far longer than carbon steel tools. Jerry Glaser in the USA produces a range of tools, mostly gouges, that keep a sharp cutting edge much longer than most – I estimate that I sharpen them once for every six times I have to sharpen a normal gouge – and these are made from cast A-11 high-speed steel. They are much more expensive, but on the grounds of less tool wear and time away from the lathe they are very cost effective.

Gouges

These are used in both spindle and headstock turnery. They are very different in section and bevel angle, and come in two types – standard, and long and strong. The term 'standard' refers to gouges that have a constant metal thickness; 'long and strong', as the term implies, is used for longer gouges, where the metal is thicker and much heavier in the base of the radius. A wide range of sizes is available.

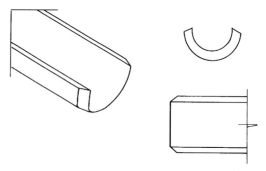

Fig 5 Between centre roughing gouge

Spindle-work roughing-out gouges are usually ¾in (18mm) to 1¼in (31mm) standard strength of deep U-section, ground square across with a 45 degree angle. They are excellent for shaping shallow curves and are used with a slicing cut to produce a finish akin to a skew.

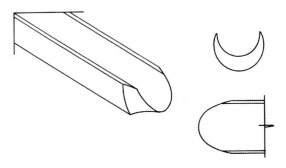

Fig 6 Spindle gouge

Spindle gouges are used for all major shaping for in between centre work. They are ground to the shape of a lady's fingernail, usually with a 30 degree angle.

Traditionally forged and shallow in section, the modern trend is for them to be made from round bar with more metal mass in the base of the radius. Traditional shallow, flatter types are normally from ¼in (6mm) to 1¼in (31mm), although I have seen these up to 3in (75mm) wide. The round bar type start from 1⁄16in (1.5mm) for miniatures and are seldom found larger than ⅝in (15mm).

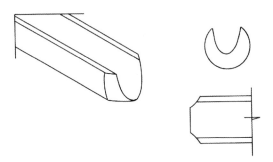

Fig 7 Bowl gouge

Bowl gouges have a much deeper flute cut in them, usually of a U- or V-section, and are traditionally ground square across, with a 45 degree angle. Recently, turners have tended to grind the wings back to create more of a fingernail shape, and V-section gouges have to be ground this way or they will not cut efficiently. I use both types, but for different things: I make aggressive roughing cuts with a gouge with the wings ground back, and refining cuts with the square-across grind, particularly on flat work, shallow gentle curve bowls and flatter sectioned deep bowls. The U-section gouge can be ground for this kind of use, but will also work with the wings ground back. Most of my gouges are ground more acutely than is normal, 55–65 degrees being common, and the reasons for these adaptations are explained more fully in the Techniques section (see pages 43-4).

Key gouge

This hybrid gouge is made from a round bar spindle gouge. I developed this tool twenty years ago, and it has many uses. The three major ones are: first, for end-grain boring and hollowing; second, instead of a skew chisel on centre work for difficult woods, when it gives a superior finish; and third, as the final cutting tool on the outside of 95 per cent of the bowls I make. They are made in ⅜in (9mm) and ½in (12mm) sizes, with a round-nosed 60–65 degree stubby angle at the tip and with a long curved, almost vertical grind on the right-hand side.

I am a great believer in modifying tools. Anything that enables you to achieve your objectives more easily, as long as it is safe and efficient, is acceptable.

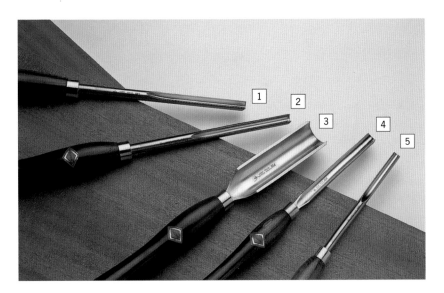

Range of gouges manufactured by Henry Taylor: ⅝in (15mm) superflute bowl gouge (1), ½in (12mm) traditional bowl gouge (2), 1½in (38mm) between centre roughing gouge (3), ¾in (18mm) traditionally forged spindle gouge (4), and ½in (12mm) spindle gouge from round bar (5)

Chisels

There are two kinds of chisel – square ended and skew ended – and they are the tools many hobby turners find the most difficult to master as well as being among the most misused of all tools.

Used correctly, chisels are capable of producing the cleanest surface possible in spindle turning. The choice of skew or square end often depends on a turner's preference or the type of work being undertaken. I prefer to use the square end for planing cuts and the skew end for most others. End grain, V-cuts and convex cuts are made with the point leading, while conical, convex and any planing cuts are made with the heel leading.

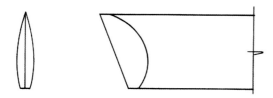

Fig 8 Oval skew chisel

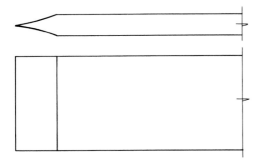

Fig 9 Square chisel, bevel ground at 40–50 degree angle

The development of oval skews in recent years has been a major step forward. Most people seem to gain confidence in using these far more quickly than they do the traditional flat-faced, square-edge type. As a rule, the skew has a cutting edge of 60–70 degrees, with a concave ground bevel on both sides of 40–50 degrees, an angle that applies also to the square end. They are normally ground straight across on the leading edge, but I prefer them to have a convex form.

Parting tools

The three main kinds of parting tool are standard, diamond-point and fluted. Their main use is for cutting deep grooves, parting components from each other or separating work from the remaining waste. They should all be used with an arcing, pivoting, peeling motion.

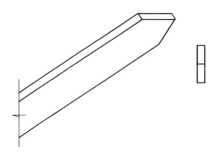

Fig 10 $\frac{1}{8}$in (3mm) high-speed steel parting tool used for small items and material saving

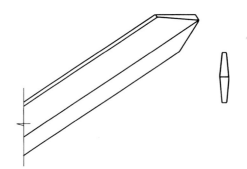

Fig 11 $\frac{3}{16}$in (5mm) high-speed steel diamond parting tool. Perhaps the most versatile with good clearance

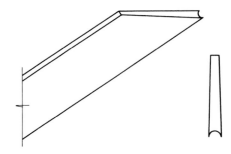

Fig 12 $\frac{3}{16}$in (5mm) high-speed fluted parting tool, gives excellent finish used with the flute down, but can mark the tool rest

The standard style is available in a number of parallel widths, from $\frac{1}{16}$in (1.5mm) to $\frac{3}{8}$in (9mm). These can bind in deep cuts, unless clearance is given. The widest parting tool is often used, like a small chisel, to roll beads or execute detail work. The widest part of a diamond-point is in the centre of the tool, which means it always affords good clearance and does not bind. Fluted parting tools are used with the flute downwards, which can put nicks in your rest, so use tape or a plastic sleeve to help prevent this. The flute is the widest part of the tool, at $\frac{5}{32}$in (4mm), so binding is not a problem. These parting tools cut end grain more cleanly than all other parting tools, and they form small beads perfectly.

Key parting tool
This is similar in shape to the fluted tool, but without the flute. It is narrower – $\frac{3}{32}$in (2mm) – to minimize grain mismatch in boxes and is tapered so there is no binding.

Scrapers
These are available in many forms, shapes and sizes. They are made from flat section steel in standard and heavy weights. Standard section is $\frac{3}{16}$–$\frac{1}{4}$in (5–6mm), while the heavy type are $\frac{3}{8}$in (9mm) thick. Heavy scrapers are usually used on larger work, or where there is tool overhang from the rest. Their thickness adds strength and damps down vibration. These are the only tools in turnery where the bevel does not rub the work. They are tilted slightly downwards, and cutting is mostly carried out at centre height. The burr on the top edge of a tool straight from the grindstone is used to remove shavings rather than dust. (If you get dust, resharpen your scraper or a rough, torn finish will result, because the tool is blunt.) Angles are acute, unlike all other lathe tools, and my own vary from as little as 15–25 degrees.

It is possible to create all objects made on a lathe from start to finish with scrapers, but it is a long, drawn-out and unsatisfactory approach. You should learn to remove wood with the correct cutting tools and use scrapers only where necessary. The scraper should be used to remove ripples and undulations or to reach areas that have proved impossible to reach with a gouge. There are exceptions to this general rule – the hollowing out of vessels through a very small orifice, for example, or when great accuracy is required, as in pattern making.

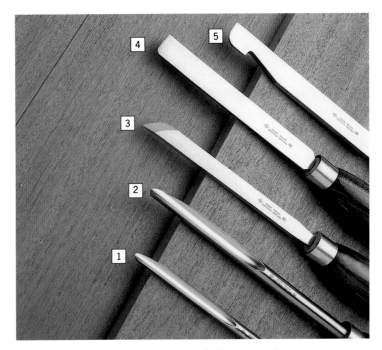

Key specialist tools manufactured by Henry Taylor: $\frac{3}{8}$in (9mm) modified spindle gouge (1), $\frac{1}{2}$in (12mm) modified spindle gouge (2), long angle skew used for detail work (3), square-ended side- and end-cutting scraper (4) and side-cutting round-nosed scraper (5)

Key modified tools manufactured by Henry Taylor: 1$\frac{1}{2}$in (38mm) French curve scraper (1), 1in (25mm) French curve scraper (2), diamond shear scraper (3), round cutaway scraper (4) and narrow parting tool (5)

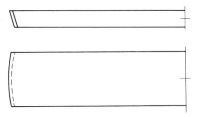

Fig 13 Square-ended scraper. Should be slightly convex to avoid dig-in

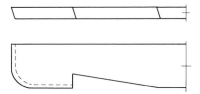

Fig 14 Side-cutting round-nosed scraper, used inside boxes and small bowls, particularly when bellied

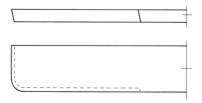

Fig 15 Side-cutting scraper, ground for use when making straight-sided and flat-bottomed boxes

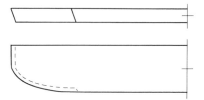

Fig 16 Key French curve scraper for removing ripples in bowls

Hook and ring tools

In this general overview of turning tools, it is possible to refer only briefly to hook or ring tools, which are much favoured in Europe and Scandinavia for end-grain work and, at times, bowls.

There are specialist tools available for hollow vessels with cranked shafts, hookers, swing wing tips and adjustable cover cutters as well as chatter tools, coning tools, bowl nesting jigs, shear scrapers and so on. All these have become part of the turner's armoury in recent years, and there is a constant stream of new products coming on

to the market, not all of which are good or some so similar to others that they have little merit.

Miscellaneous tools and accessories

All general hand woodworking tools will be found to be useful at some time to the turner. Hammers, mallets, saws, chisels, drill bits and screwdrivers are among the most useful, but the turner also needs and uses a number of tools not normally found in a general woodwork kit.

Cone tool

The pick of the specialist tools that have recently become available has to be the Kel McNaughton System for bowl centre saving. The ingenious jig and cutters make it more versatile than and superior to all the other devices that have been invented and used over the years.

Cone tool specially made for bowl centre saving

Calipers

Calipers of all types and sizes will be found to be indispensable. Outside calipers will be the most useful for checking diameters and wall thickness; inside calipers are needed for checking the apertures of hollow items.

More specialist calipers, such as double-ended ones, transfer the measurements from one end to the other. These are used where standard ones are difficult to use or cannot reach. Some offer both an inside and outside measuring facility, and calipers of this type are mainly used on large bowls and hollow vessels.

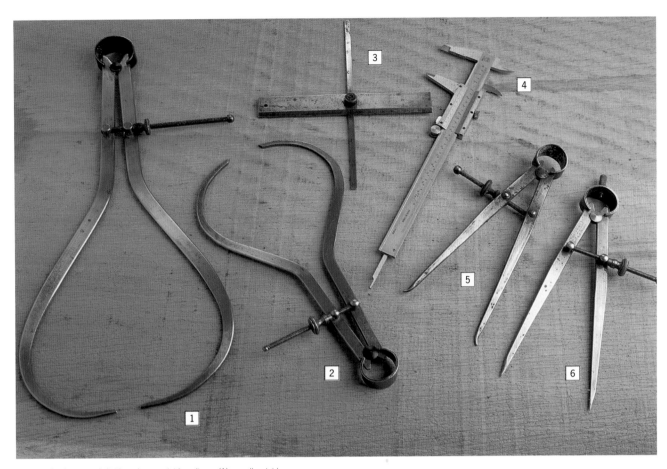

A range of calipers and dividers: large outside calipers (1), small outside calipers (2), depth gauge (3), vernier (4), inside calipers (5) and dividers (6)

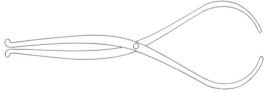

Fig 17 Double-ended inside and outside calipers

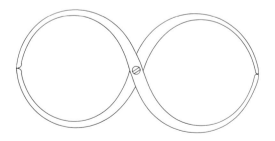

Fig 18 Double-ended outside calipers

More specialist calipers allow you to take a measurement where the other kinds would not.

These are closed down on the area you wish to measure in the normal way, but an extra-small arm that is part of the caliper is locked, the main caliper re-opened, and then closed down again to the locked small arm, giving an accurate measurement. In the trade they are known as 'tell tales'.

Dividers and pairs of compasses
Dividers have two metal points; pairs of compasses have one metal point and a pencil (pairs of wing compasses have two metal points). Some have fine thread adjustment, while others have an arm with a lock nut. They are used for marking out bowl blanks or any disc to be cut for mounting on the lathe, and for transferring measurements to any rotary stock on the lathe.

Depth gauge
A depth gauge is essential for checking the depth of anything that you may accidentally go through the bottom of.

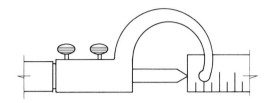

Fig 19 Setting dimension for sizing tool

Sizing tool
Used with the beading/parting tool, a sizing tool will allow you to cut constant diameters. It is excellent for component production work that needs tenons, and, once set, you have no need for calipers.

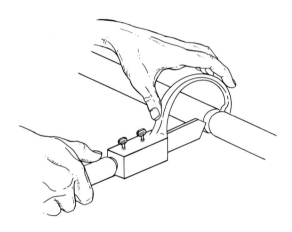

Fig 20 Sizing tool in use

Centre finder
A centre finder will allow you to find a precise centre in seconds on round, square, hexagonal and octagonal stock.

Depth drill
A long-shafted drill mounted in a handle is very useful for setting a depth, especially in bowls. You push the drill directly in the centre of the work while it is rotating on the lathe and mark the depth required on the drill.

Bradawl
This small pointed instrument is a must for marking centres.

Calico mop
Mounted on a mandrel in the lathe, these mops are excellent for buffing the surface of a turned object to impart lustre.

Cyano-acrylate glue
This comes in different consistencies – water-thin, syrupy and honey-like – but the most often used are the thin and the syrupy types. The thin glue can be used for filling hairline gaps, adhering bark and so on, while the syrupy glue is used for mounting block work (use accelerator on one face, glue on the other), for filling small gaps with wood dust or powder mix or, when used with the accelerator, for gluing brass to wood.

Steel rules
Their use is obvious, but it is advisable to have a range of sizes, with both metric and imperial measurements.

Electric drills
These are used mostly for power sanding and for drilling the odd hole. Industrial quality drills are best, with the two-speed setting type being less prone to wear than the dialled variable type. Hair-trigger finger variables are fine. When they are used for power-sanding, 2000rpm plus is required, and mine are capable of 2200–2800rpm.

Jig saw
A jig saw is useful for cross-cutting thin boards that would be difficult to handle on the band saw or when the length required is greater than the throat of the band saw.

Orbital sander
I have two good small palm sanders (Makita and Dewalt), which I use for sanding the base of the only item I make that is not reversed chucked (chopping board). Because this article has a planed base, sanding in this way gives a fine finish.

Heat gun
A heat gun is useful for those who wet-turn finished products. It can be used to dry a surface before sanding.

Battery drill/screw driver

A battery-operated tool with good torque is invaluable for securing faceplates and faceplate rings to blanks.

Angle grinder

This item is useful if you are into sculpural work. I have a 4½in (115mm) one that I use with an Arbotech blade for rapid wood removal and decorative work.

Power carver

This tool fits into my pillar drill and has a flexible shaft. I use the hand-held carving head to create decorative effects on a range of bowls, vessles and other items.

Chain saw

A good electric chain saw is useful for breaking down large sections of wood that are too heavy to handle, for cutting out natural bowl blanks from logs and so on. Take care when you use a chain saw and make sure you use safety equipment.

Router

A router is a useful acquisition in any wood workshop, though non-essential. One of its many functions is illustrated in making the salt and sugar spoons in the project section of this book (see page 80).

Other machinery

I regard some machines as essential – namely, a good band saw and bench grinder. Others items, like a pillar drill and disc/belt sander, are normally to be found in the turner's workshop, and mine is no exception. I also have a planer/thicknesser, which has become essential, and a circular saw, which I seldom use.

Band saw

Buy the best you can afford and the biggest you can fit into your workshop – you won't regret it. I use a two-wheel, floor-standing machine with a 1½hp (1.1kW) motor with fingertip adjustment blade guides above and below the table, and revolving bearings for the back of the blade to run against.

Although my present saw is good, the capacity needs to be bigger, because the 9½in (242mm) depth of cut and 15¾in (400mm) throat are restricting at times, making it necessary to cut items with a chain saw that I would rather cut on the band saw. However, it enables me to meet 90 per cent of my requirements quite efficiently, especially when it is fitted with a four-skip, blue, flexi-back blade.

Bench grinder

A double-ended bench-grinder is a must. Do not buy one that takes wheel stones less than 6in (150mm) in diameter or less than ¾in (18mm) wide, and make sure that the machine is powerful. The wheels should be white aluminium oxide with a vitrified bond, which will provide faster, cooler sharpening because the granulated abrasive particles are bonded in such a way that they wear off and provide a fresh grinding surface.

My machine is fitted with 7in (175mm) diameter wheels, 1in (25mm) wide, of 100 grit and 60 grit. It has a ⅓hp (0.2kW) induction motor that runs at 2900rpm, and although sixteen years old, it performs quite adequately.

Pillar drill

If you make a lot of items that require drilling, a pillar drill (drill press in the USA) will be essential. If you drill only occasionally, you can do this on the lathe.

Sanding disc/belt sander

There are many products that can be made on the lathe for which a disc or belt sander can be of great use. At one time, I regarded this as an essential part of my workshop equipment, but over the years my product range has changed and I hardly use one now.

Planer/thicknesser

The planer/thicknesser is a recent addition to my workshop, but I cannot now do without it.

HEALTH AND SAFETY

This is an area that demands that you pay considerable attention, whether it is the air you breathe or the layout of your workshop. It is difficult to mention everything that makes for safe and efficient workshop conditions but some advice will be helpful.

It goes without saying that the general level of lighting in your workshop should be good, with local lights at each lathe – I use two spring-loaded desk lights to provide directional light. It is also essential to keep a good first aid kit and fire extinguishers in your workshop.

Lung and eye protection

I make no secret of the fact I do not like wearing things on my head or face, but I do, and so should you.

Face masks
These are the minimum requirement for anyone who turns wood. They vary from the simple Martindale through to very sophisticated ones with changeable filters.

Goggles
These should have side eye protection to stop chips flying into the eye from the side. I often wear them over my normal prescription glasses when demonstrating in public.

Face shield
A shield affords full face and eye protection and is better than goggles.

Respirator helmets
There are many styles and makes of these on the market, but all seem to do a good job. They are powered by rechargeable batteries, which run for four to eight hours, and they provide a constant down draft of clean air, affording both lung and eye protection in one unit. They are superior to anything so far mentioned. Turners who wear spectacles will find them excellent, as there is no danger of your glasses getting steamed up, as happens with most other masks.

Dust extractors
I installed a dust/chip extractor in my workshop after developing breathing difficulties. Within six weeks of having a dust extractor installed, this problem was no more. There are many systems, from shaker, oil drum to the most common drop bag (which is the sort I have). All, however, suck air, heat and dust from the workshop. Some, especially the oil drum type, are very noisy, but it is best if all types of units are enclosed and installed outside the workshop. If they have to be inside, build a sound-proofed enclosure, vented to the outside, allowing motor heat and fine dust particles to escape. This is the arrangement I have. I have 6in (150mm) round metal ducting from the extractor linked to three lathes and my band saw; the ducting narrows at points to 4in (100mm). There are blast gates at strategic points within the system, and the planer is hooked to the system as required.

I now have two suction outlets from each lathe – for years I had one. Some are in 4in (100mm) Stayput hose (which, as the name implies, is what it does); others are in flexible hose with PVC rainwater hopper heads attached. This latter arrangement incurs about 5 per cent of the cost of purpose-built metal systems but does the job just as well. Despite the excellence of this system, when I power sand larger items I wear a respirator helmet as well. It is not worth risking lung damage.

Fans
Although they are not as effective as a purpose-built dust extractor, an extractor or squirrel-caged fan, window- or wall-mounted behind the lathe to suck out the air, will help. They are fine in summer but not so good in winter. In many hot countries, people can work with their workshop doors open and with a fan positioned behind the turner so that the dust is blown outside.

Electronic air cleaners
Good cleaners will remove 96 per cent of airborne dust, smoke and pollen particles in 60 to 90 seconds. I suspect one of these fitted in conjunction with a good extractor would be the ultimate workshop solution to dust.

GENERAL SAFETY POINTS

Most safety in the workshop is common sense.

- Make sure that the space around any machine is clear of loose cables, bits of wood and so on – anything, in fact, that you could fall or trip over.
- Clear up shavings regularly and remove them from the workshop.
- Keep rags that have been used to apply certain polishes and oils in an airtight container because they can sometimes self combust.
- Keep steel wool well away from grinders and out of line of anywhere sparks might fly. It can smoulder for a very long time before combusting.
- Stand on a good rubber-backed carpet or mat, especially if you work on a concrete floor – it is easier on the feet and legs.
- Always work with sharp tools. Accidents are more likely to happen with blunt ones.
- Position your grinder a few feet from the lathe so that you have to walk a little to it to help circulate the blood in the legs. Standing in one place all the time is not good for you.
- If you feel tired, stop turning. Accidents are more likely to happen when you are tired.
- Never turn or use any other machine if you have drunk any alcohol.

At the lathe
- When you mount wood in the lathe, always make sure it is well secured on the faceplate, on the glue block (glue cured), in the chuck or between centres before starting to work.
- Always remember to rotate the work by hand before switching on the lathe (set at the correct speed) to make sure that it is secure and clears the tool rest as well as that the cross-slide is locked in position

- When work is mounted between centres, make sure that the tailstock is locked in position and that the spindle is locked in its spline.
- Set a lathe speed that errs on the slower side. You can always speed things up, but if you start too fast, both lathe and work can vibrate badly and, in extreme cases, fly from the lathe. The advent of variable speed lathes makes speed selection easier to get right and to get wrong. If you have been working on small diameter work at high speeds and are going to leave the lathe and workshop for a while, turn the speed selection down before leaving the room. This is a good habit to get into at the end of each working day.
- When you mount a new block of wood in the lathe that is out of true or unbalanced, stand out of line when you first switch on the lathe.
- Always remove tailstock centres from the lathe when you are working on end-grain hollowing or any form of headstock work. It is easy to knock and damage your elbows on these.
- Do not leave chuck keys and levers in chucks mounted on the lathe.
- Wear a smock, overalls or an apron. All should be high-fitting around the neck to stop shavings and chippings from finding their way into uncomfortable places.
- Roll your sleeves back, tuck in your tie (better still, don't wear one), do not wear loose clothing or jewellery or have anything dangling near any machine. Long hair (even long beards) should be tied back.

TIMBER

I love working with wood. There are thousands of different types and species, but most of us will only work with a relatively small number of these. Over the years I have worked with over 150 species of wood, but I use a much more limited range on a day-to-day basis. Part of the fascination of working with wood is that almost every piece cuts, turns and finishes differently – some are a real joy, while others bring great frustration.

If you buy a reasonably sized log that has been field or hedgerow grown, it will have many variances; the grain might be open, tight, straight or interlocked; there may be rippled figure in the pressure growth areas, near the branch and root spurs. If you can, obtain some crotch figure, where the trunk forks or branches break out from the main trunk, provided the tree is converted correctly. There are also the popular grain formations such as burrs, quilts, fiddlebacks, bird's-eyes, the wonderful quarter-sawn figure of some woods, plus the spalting caused by fungal attack that is very attractive.

As a rule, mild, straight-grown species that work relatively easily are best selected for production-type turnery. This is a competitive market, where all costs are relevant. Anything that slows down the making process must be avoided, and this is why the more flamboyantly figured woods are normally found in individual work, where time and material costs are not such critical factors. Highly figured woods are often more challenging to work with, but your aims are different – each object is crafted to be aesthetically pleasing and stimulating. Form and shape become of paramount importance in this sort of work, but there remains no doubt that if the object is made from highly figured wood, it will sell more quickly and for a higher price. Remember that wood can be highly seductive, so choose selectively. Decorative figure is best used for larger items. When it is used for smaller ones it is often far too dominant.

BUYING

These days I buy almost all my wood from two sources, northern temperate timber from one, imported stock from another. I have developed a good working relationship with both suppliers, and they phone me when they have something special they think will interest me. They also look out for things if I ask them to. If you can build this sort of relationship with a supplier it is very beneficial and will make your life a little easier.

Country sawmills

Timber buying has changed dramatically over the years. Gone for the most part are those wonderful old country sawmills, which were happy to sell or even give you the odd block or board. I used to spend days in these places, poking about and unearthing the odd gem at a give-away price. If you still have one near you, you can learn a great deal, especially if you can take a good look at the logs and timber stacks with one of the old workers in the yard. This can be the first step you take in developing an instinctive ability to recognize what to look for. This is a difficult area to teach anyone, especially because each tree is different, but there are obvious guidelines. Every variety has its own special characteristics, but just when you think you know a thing or two about a certain timber, a log will come along that knocks all the known rules on the head. This is all part of the fascination of wood, and even the most knowledgeable person will, at some time or other, be surprised by some trick nature has played.

Supermarkets

Many hobby woodturners will, I suspect, buy their wood pre-cut and packaged, in hot-waxed sealed squares and discs, just as they buy cheese from the supermarket. The label bears the timber's name, the price and the seasoned state. (Incidentally, terms like 'part dry' or 'part seasoned' should be interpreted as wet.) This is an expensive way of buying timber, but if you do not have good conversion equipment, like a chain saw or decent band saw, you will have little choice. At least there should be no wastage, and I must admit that I buy squares of exotic timbers for boxes, mainly because that is the only way you can buy certain types of wood these days.

Other sources

There are many other sources of supply, although they are more variable and less consistent. However, all avenues are worth pursuing at times. Local tree surgeons, neighbours, landscape gardeners, building-site developers, farmers and council park departments all fell trees at various times, and it is worth asking what is going to happen to them. All too often they are cut up for logs, taken to a dump or burned on site. If you are lucky, you may get the timber for nothing or for a modest price.

Buying planks

If you go to a timber yard, keep a look out for the odd plank with some wild or unusual grain. You can often buy these more cheaply than straight, mild-grained pieces, but if the plank has an unusual figure throughout, you will have to pay a premium price.

There are differences between imported planks and those milled in the UK. Almost all imported planks come square-edged and bark- and sap-free. Most UK timber is milled through and through, with the sapwood and bark left on, or with one square edge. Exceptions are for structural timbers, fence and gate posts or at the request of a customer.

When you go to look at a stack of timber, many

Burr maple

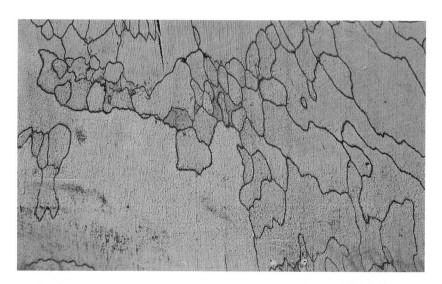

Spalted beech

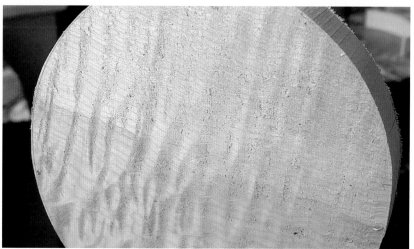

Rippled maple

Bird's-eye maple

Wood can be bought in a range of different plank sizes and sections depending on your requirements. This is a mixture of imported and home-grown wood

merchants will try to sell you the top board. This will seldom be the best, and you should insist on looking through the stack to find what you really want. Look out for a plank that offers you a good range of size options for items you produce on a regular basis, with as little wastage as possible. If the plank is from UK-milled stock, remember to make an allowance for sapwood wastage. The wastage will vary from species to species, but a 2–3in (50–75mm) waste factor would be average on most planks.

Because they are square-edged, you do not need to make an allowance for wastage when you buy imported woods, and you will usually find a wide range of sizes available with little wastage. You will, however, normally pay a much higher price than for UK-grown timber.

Exotic woods

The word 'exotic' conjures up all sorts of images, but Dale Nish's comment perhaps best sums things up: 'an exotic wood is an ordinary piece of wood a long way from home.' That said, some woods are definitely exotic, and dealing with them takes you into another world – and price. Their characteristics – colour, texture, figure, smell, stability and so on – can be very seductive, but I urge you to wait until your skills are at a level where you can do justice to

these wonderful materials. The use of some of these woods is controversial, and it is up to each individual to decide to use them. I use them in a small part of my work and find they bring another dimension to it. However, whatever your view about their use, please do not use them until you can make beautiful objects out of them.

CONVERSION AND STORAGE

Most of the timber you obtain free is likely to be in the form of small logs, probably 6–12in (150–300mm) in diameter. If you are into wet turning, the only real problem you have is finding the time to work your material before it starts to dry out and loses the elasticity of the sap.

If you wish to work the wood dry, conversion of some kind will be best. If this is not possible at the time, leave the log in as long a section as possible and seal the ends with end seal, oil-based paint or tar to slow down the drying process and minimize end-splitting. You will have to accept there may be a certain amount of radial cracking in small logs.

If you have a small log with a diameter of, say, 8in (200mm), it is usual to box out the central pith and disregard the sapwood. By doing this you are likely to obtain only quite small pieces.

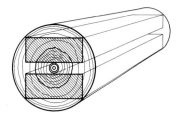

Fig 21 Log divided for small planks

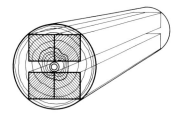

Fig 22 Log divided for squares

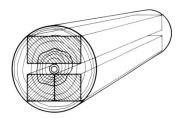

Fig 23 Log divided for planks and squares

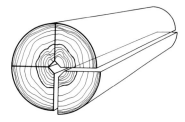

Fig 24 Log divided into quarters

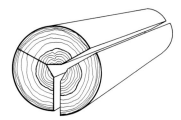

Fig 25 Log divided into thirds

The line drawings illustrate some ways in which the log can be divided into planks and squares, and your yield will be in the region of 2½in (64mm) squares and 5 x 2½in (125 x 64mm) planks.

The seasoning time of your converted timber will depend on the storage conditions. In general, the adage 'year to the inch' can be disregarded when you are dealing with sizes like these. If possible, store the wood away from direct sunlight and high winds, at least in the early stages of the drying process. A covered area with a gentle air movement is ideal. Place wooden bearers on the floor and start to stack your timber. Thin wooden stickers should be placed horizontally at intervals of about 24in (610mm) between each plank or square to allow air to pass around each piece so that gradual drying will take place. As a guide, in the UK the squares are likely to be dry in six to nine months and the planks in eighteen months. Remember that air-dried timber is unlikely to have less than a 16 to 20 per cent moisture content. Most homes have central heating, with a moisture content of around 10 per cent, so all timbers should be in the warmer workshop for a month or two before use. Larger pieces should, of course, be left in the workshop for longer than this.

Quick seasoning

Squares can be turned into cylinders, and if they are going to be used to make articles like condiment sets, pepper mills and napkin rings, you can drill out some of the centre to speed drying. Ovalling will take place, and the holes will need to be redrilled true, but the drying time will have been reduced to weeks instead of months.

Rough-turning of bowls while wet has been going on for centuries – I have turned thousands this way – and when they are dry they are remounted for final shaping and finishing. There is some distortion when you work like this, and you need to increase the size to allow for shrinkage. As a guide, a finished bowl with a diameter of 10in (255mm) should be rough-turned initially about ¾in (18mm) larger.

Shrinkage can be avoided by the use of PEG (polyethylene glycol). Items rough-turned when wet are immersed in a tank of the diluted solution at a set temperature. A process of osmosis leads to the sap in the

Radial cracks are typical in
small logs

wood being replaced by the chemical, and this stops
shrinkage and distortion. The immersion lasts for eight to
ten weeks, and you need to stir the tank every day. Drain
the immersed items for a few days after removing them
from the tank, and be prepared for a total change in the
character of the wood. A finish that is impervious to
moisture, such as polyurethane, must be used or the work
will feel greasy and clammy because the wood cannot
absorb atmospheric moisture. I am not a lover of the
process, but it does have many uses. PEG is used to
preserve ancient archaeological finds of wood and leather
by museums – artefacts from the *Mary Rose* are preserved
in this way – but the molecular structure is different from
what woodturners use, even though it is essentially the
same material.

Other drying methods

Many turners who produce large volumes of bowls use
dehumidifying chambers to hasten the drying process
after rough-turning. Depending on the timber species and
moisture content, a drying time-cycle of anywhere between
thirty and forty-five days can be expected when using
these chambers.

Microwaving on the defrost setting is another option

for the odd piece if you are in a hurry. Trial and error will
tell you what you can get away with but, as a general
rule, a wall thickness over 1in (25mm) should be
avoided. A number of short bursts in the oven is a good
method to use. Wet, thin turned work can be
manipulated to shape when hot and pliable, but be
careful not to burn your hands.

Boiling the sap out of bowls is another possibility after
rough-turning. Again, you will learn by trial and error how
long different species require. Wash the bowls under cold
running water after boiling. And remember to expect some
colour loss from some species when using this process.

Absorption drying in paper sacks (such as those used
for packing potatoes) is a slow method but may be the only
choice if you are working with tricky woods that might
crack when exposed to too much air or heat during the
drying cycle. Turn the bags inside out from time to time to
stop mildew and mould forming.

T E C H N I Q U E S

Although everyone has a slightly different approach to turning, my view is that you should develop skills and techniques that allow you to work safely, speedily and efficiently. The methods described throughout this book are based on this premise, and they are the ones I use to earn my living.

There are several areas in turning that have similarities to driving a car or to sport. This may seem an odd statement to make, but think about it.

Grip

The grip of a steering wheel, club, racquet or bat is very important, and so is that on turning tools. Here the similarity continues, for most people, when they grip a steering wheel or a sporting implement for the first time, hold on as though their lives depended on it, gripping so hard that their knuckles turn white. Yes, you must grip, but in a relaxed manner that gives control to guide, not force; otherwise, you will be tense and rigid, tiring quickly and with a tendency to overreact. Your movements will be jerky instead of fluid, and this will be apparent in your work.

Stance

The way you stand is also vitally important. It is best if your feet are positioned so that you need to move them as little as possible during all cutting operations, instead moving your body from the ankles. To achieve this, your body weight needs to be distributed over the foot where cutting begins, transferring to where the cutting ends.

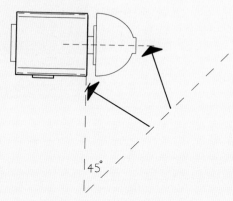

Fig 26 Foot position for turning outside of a bowl

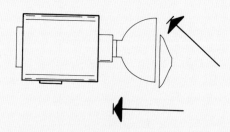

Fig 27 Foot position for turning inside of a bowl

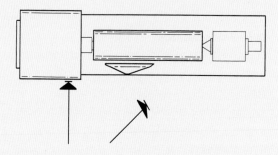

Fig 28 Foot position for general spindle turning

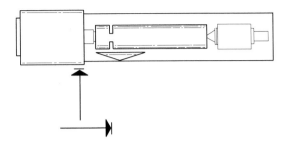

Fig 29 Foot position for parting cuts at headstock end

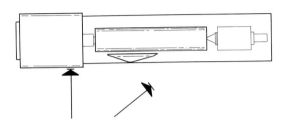

Fig 30 Foot position for parting cuts at tailstock end

This will not be possible when you are turning long spindles, but try to turn in as long and flowing a way as you can. Most headstock work should allow you to turn in the suggested manner. In general, headstock turning calls for a front-on approach, while spindle turning requires a more side-on approach. The foot positions indicated by arrows in the drawings show the sort of thing to aim for, and if you adopt these, you will find your body is pretty much in the position I advocate. Using the body to give added support to tool handles during much of the cutting movements gives you greater control of the tools than can be gained by hand control alone.

Profiles

The form of the outside of any object is best assessed by looking across the profile being created, near the top of its rotation in the lathe. A piece of card positioned behind the work can often be of help, as it blocks out any clutter that may distract the eye. If you try to view the shape where the cutting is being done, there are any number of distractions for the eye, from the tool, to your hand, the rest and so on. Just like driving, it is about looking ahead and anticipating.

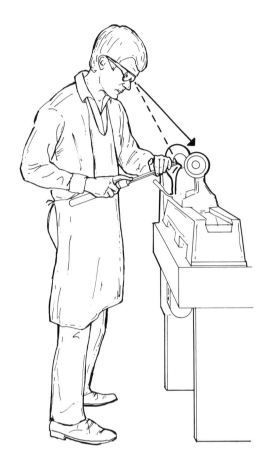

Fig 31 Eye direction for profile forming

Bowl gouges

Most headstock work should be done with a gouge. The gouges I use have bevels of 55–65 degrees, rather than the normally recommended 45 degree angles. This initially came about by mistake rather than design, through lazy grinding when I sharpened too much of the leading edge and not enough of the heel. I have now been grinding these shorter bevel angles for years on purpose, and I find they allow much more fluid use of the tool, particularly when I am hollowing a bowl's interior. The initial entry cut is slightly less easy, but almost any shape can be cut from the top to the centre of the base in one flowing, continuous movement, with the bevel rubbing in support of the cut throughout. I can also use the gouges in a more horizontal plane than

Fingers supporting the rim of a bowl

would be possible with a conventionally ground gouge. Those with bedded lathes will find this of great benefit, because pieces of larger diameters can be tackled before the handle fouls the bed.

Scrapers

The scraper (see pages 29–30) is a necessary tool, but its use should be strictly limited in conventional turning. There should be no need to use them for more than 5 to 10 per cent of headstock work, and then they should be used to skim ripples or unevenness from a surface, not for major shaping. Keep them on the move and take light, passing cuts.

Conventionally, scrapers are presented flat on the rest and cut at centre height. They are also tilted downwards, 10–15 degrees out of the horizontal, which means the tool rest is set higher than for gouge use.

Shear scraping will give a cleaner cut on most surfaces than conventional scraping, but greater control and skill are needed, because the scraper is used at angles from 45 to 30 degrees out of the vertical.

My own view is that scrapers have no function at all in spindle turning. I think gouges and chisels should be used throughout.

Support and steadying

If you are right-handed, the left hand plays the supporting role in most turning, and often only the thumb is in contact with the tool on the rest. As final shaping takes place and the object becomes thinner, the fingers of the left hand steady the piece, absorbing vibration or preventing flexing. This is particularly the case with the walls of bowls (see photograph above) and flanges of platters and dishes in headstock turning.

In spindle work, a steadying action is, again, the aim, and it often counteracts the pressure of the cutting tools being applied in a forwards movement. Slicing cuts should be made in the direction of the tail- and headstock to minimize whip and flexing on thin work.

The right hand is the one that dictates the depth, direction and angle of cut. You will develop a strong right wrist, which will enable you to make positive, controlled fluid movements.

Often long, thin spindles call for more support than the hand alone can afford. Steadies range from the simple shop-made sliding weighted wedge steadies through to the sophisticated ones of today, that support large hollow forms on 'rollerblade' wheels.

Roughing a spindle with a ¾in (18mm) gouge

Planing a cylinder with the heel of a skew chisel. The fingers of the left hand are wrapped round the cylinder to support and steady

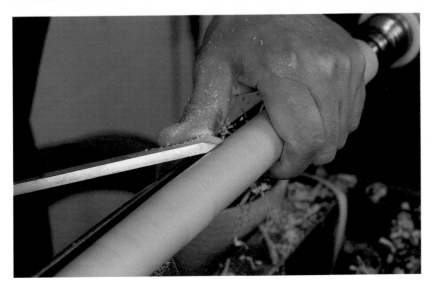

Planing a cylinder with a square-ended chisel

Fingers supporting under a thin spindle to prevent whipping while using the heel of a skew chisel

Problem grain

When you are dealing with a difficult grain area that tears or pecks within a piece, the application of some finishing oil or soft wax can have a magical effect, for it will soften the fibres and allow them to be cut with a great deal less trouble. Oil is the more effective, because it penetrates more easily, but it should be avoided if your final finish is cellulose lacquer based, because a chemical reaction to the oil residue will take place, causing a white, blotchy finish. If this is your intended finish, use paste wax instead of oil. Push the wax into the torn fibres with your thumb or fingers. The penetration will be less than with oil and more than one application may be required to achieve the desired smooth surface.

Planing with a ½in (12mm) modified Key spindle gouge is recommended for difficult timbers. Again, the left hand supports and steadies the cylinder

SHARPENING

Tools must always be sharp if you are to cut wood cleanly, and if you have the slightest doubt about a tool's edge quality, sharpen it. You may feel I have a somewhat cavalier approach to sharpening, and in some respects this is true, especially when you consider that whole books have been written on the subject. The procedures outlined below are the ones that have worked for me for many years.

My only real concern is that my tools are sharp, free of multi-facets and ground to my desired shape. I have no problem at all in achieving these aims, but I know from experience that this is an area that causes the novice turner great difficulty, and there is a plethora of grinding jigs on the market because of this problem. I am not sure that, if you use these jigs, you will ever develop the skills you should to grind freehand. Freehand grinding is much quicker, and there are no adjustments to make to the tool rest and no jig angles to set up. However, if you need, or prefer, to use a jig, then so be it.

The angles of bevels are not of great importance to me. Many turners feel that if an angle is not exactly as described in some publication or another it will be almost impossible to use that tool, and they spend a great deal of time trying to achieve the precise angles that have been recommended. Of course, certain angles do help, and the degree of variance possible is less with chisels and spindle gouges, but they are not critical, because you can easily compensate for any variation by lowering and raising the tool handle, thus still allowing the bevel to rub supporting the cutting edge.

Wheels

I grind all my tools on aluminium oxide wheels. These have a vitrified bond, which allows for fast, cool grinding of my high-speed steel tools. You should forget about carborundum wheels for high-speed steel: the harder the steel, the softer the wheel.

I use 60 grit and 100 grit, 7in (178mm) in diameter by 1in (25mm) wide, and these give me the edge I require direct from the grinder. Oilstones and slipstones have no

place in my sharpening process, although these were used a great deal before the advent of high-speed steel tools. I move from the lathe to the grinder and back to the lathe as quickly and efficiently as possible, without convex and multi-faceted bevels.

When you present the tool to the wheel, it is best if you let the heel touch first. Then lift the handle to the desired angle. Once you start to sharpen the edge, you will see sparks coming over the top of it.

Gouges

Sharpening gouges has become much easier over the years as most are now made from round bar. A square-ended bowl gouge is a very easy tool to grind: keep the heel and edge in constant contact with the stone and rotate the gouge from top edge to top edge. Having ground all the way round, you should now have a very sharp gouge with a hollow grind.

There are two ways of sharpening fingernail-shaped gouges. The first is to keep the gouge in the same place on the wheel and swing the handle through a large arc. The second is to rotate the gouge in a fixed position, but pushing the tool upwards and downwards on the wheel as you keep the heel and edge in contact with the wheel. Both methods require practice, but the first, swinging through an arc, is the easier.

Chisels

If the chisel is ground square across, you should let the heel touch first, then lower until the sparks come over the leading edge. Slide the tool across the wheel, keeping it in constant contact. At no time should you let it become stationary, as this allows heat to build up, leading to bluing and subsequent softening of the steel, which in turn causes the tools to blunt more quickly. This is no longer the problem it used to be, because carbon high-speed steel is considerably more forgiving. Do not plunge high-speed steel into cold water, but let the tool cool naturally.

Skews can be sharpened in the same way, but if you wish to have a curved shape on the blade, pivot the tool on the rest. The amount of pivot is dictated by the amount of curve you require. Both these tools are ground from both sides, so

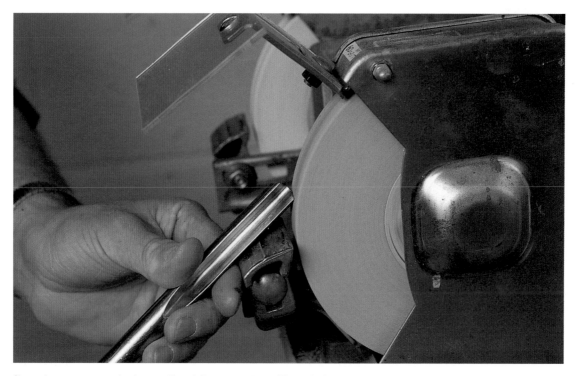

Sharpening a square across bowl gouge with a rotating movement on a 60 grit wheel

Pivoting movements in sharpening a chisel

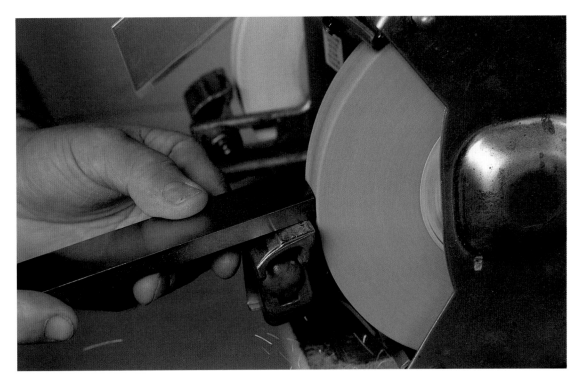

Grinding a scraper – traversing and pivoting

it is usual for a wire edge to form. Most people oilstone this off, but I prefer to drag it through a soft block of wood, which works just as well and saves stoning.

Scrapers

In order to cut, scrapers need the burr created from the grinder, so the last thing you need is an oilstone. These are the easiest tools of all to sharpen: they are applied flat on the rest and, depending on the shape, are traversed or pivoted. Just as with all the other tools, let the heel touch first, lift the handle to the angle required and, when sparks come over the edge, you know the heel and edge are in contact and good sharpening is taking place. Some people turn the scrapers upside-down to sharpen them, thus creating a greater burr. I have never felt the need for this – the conventional way creates enough burr for me.

Safety

My grinder runs at 2850rpm. It is fitted with white aluminium oxide 7in (178mm) diameter 1in (25mm) wheels. It is

securely mounted on a heavy bench with a wheel centre height of 46in (1170mm). This is the same height as my lathe spindle and provides an ideal height for grinding, with no painful back bending required and good vision when grinding the tool edge.

When using the grinder, always operate it with the manufacturer's eye spark protection shields in place. Protect your eyes with goggles if there are no shields provided. In fact it is a good policy to do so even if shields are available. A single spark can cause a very serious eye injury. It is not worth the risk of neglecting eye safety precautions.

Position the grinding wheel tool rests close to the wheels – a ¹⁄₁₆in (2mm) gap is all that is required. Do not sharpen tools on the side of the wheel as this is a dangerous practice.

At no time should you use a damaged wheel; always work safely. Do not make scrapers from old files, unless you have a sound understanding how to re-temper the steel. If this is not done they can be very brittle and snap easily. Buy good tools that are designed for the job of woodturning – it's far better to be safe than sorry.

FINISHING AND FINISHES

Finishing is an area that seems to cause many people a great deal of difficulty. There are many problems, but poor abrading and the application of finish are the two I encounter most often. The poor use of abrasives causes deep, abrasive scratch marks on a surface or the abrading away of crisp definition detail. This is often followed by the application of an inappropriate finish. The finish is sometimes thick and treacle-like, or, if the correct finish has been selected, it is distributed unevenly, resulting in a patchy, blotchy look. Unfortunately the above observations can be applied all too often to work that up until the finishing process started was quite well made. This section will be of help in these cases.

HAND ABRADING

Great advances have been made in the quality and variety of abrasive materials in recent years. I use the term abrading rather than sanding, which was the term that was used in the days when turners used sandpaper. Very few turners use sandpaper these days because its cutting edge is lost in seconds.

Garnet paper was once the best choice for the turner. Then soft-flex or super-flex silicon carbide and aluminium oxide wet and dry papers came on the market. I still use these at times, as they are still the best for fine detailing and for finishing some types of work. The advent of the flexible cloth-backed aluminium oxide abrasives, which used to be too stiff, has brought a new dimension to

Traditional hand sanding. Note the extra pressure support of the left hand

Traditional interior sanding. The left hand supports the bowl's exterior to prevent flexing.

finishing. They cut faster and last longer, and although they are more expensive, they are worth every penny. The coarsest abrasive of this type I have is 100 grit, but I seldom use it, simply because bludgeoning a finish through abrading is not my way. I have always believed that you should tool your work cleanly and abrade as little as possible. Though it may help, no amount of abrading and polishing will put poor tool work right.

I always keep 120, 150, 180, 240, 320, 400 and 500 grit in stock, and often use 0000 steel wool or ultra-fine Scotch-Brite pads after the sanding. I use more Scotch-Brite, another fairly new development, than steel wool these days.

Start with the coarsest grit deemed necessary, and let each grit do its work before you move on to the next one. Point your fingers downwards. Support thin work with one hand while abrading with the other. Fine detail sanding on headstock turning is often best done, with great care, on the upward rotation of the lathe, which gives a clearer view and results in a more detailed finish. Abrade your work either at the speed you turned at or a little slower. Do not abrade at a faster speed because this generates friction heat and can induce heat cracks. It also wears out the abrasive more quickly and does not cut as well. I also abrade with oil and wax, and this is described in the relevant sections of the projects.

POWER ABRADING

In 1973, when woodturning became my full-time living, I was told that you could power-sand things to finish on the lathe. Being a purist in those days, I viewed this as cheating. A visit to David Ellsworth's workshop in the USA in 1981 changed this view totally. On the outside of his hollow forms he used Trimite 6in (150mm), self-adhesive paper discs in grits from 150 down to 700, mounted on various foam-backed pads. The discs were obtained from automobile finishing workshop suppliers on rolls of a hundred, and these are also available in Britain.

There are three main advantages to this method: first, speed; second, less friction heat; and finally, fewer abrasive scratch marks. The only drawback is dust, making a good dust extraction system and a respirator helmet essential.

The system that David employed was fine for what he did, but not for what I had in mind: I needed a smaller system. I contacted a company in Birmingham that was able to supply Abra-discs in 1in (25mm), 2in (50mm) and 3in (75mm) diameters. These were hard rubber discs with a 1in (25mm), semi-hard foam rubber face, and a ¼in (6mm) shaft, which was bonded into the hard rubber backing body and could be held in an electric drill. Unfortunately, the abrasive discs mounted on the rubber pads had a very variable adhesive backing and only went

Power-sanding the outside of
a large bowl with the Velcro
(touch-and-close fastener)
system

Power-sanding the interior
of the bowl with the same
system

down to 240. Sometimes the discs stayed on for only a few seconds, and sometimes they were difficult to get off. There was nothing wrong with the pads; it was the adhesive. This problem was finally resolved, thanks to the entrepreneurial Nick Davidson, with a Velcro gripping system. Cloth-backed abrasives from 60 grit to 400 grit were available. This system is now used in most parts of the world by hobby turners and professionals alike, and it is still my favourite power-sanding system. The best pads come from Australia and these are what I use.

I also sometimes use a more aggressive power-lock system, which has no foam face, but is just a hard pad and hard twist locking disc. The latest system, called Grip-a-Disc, puts a ¼in (6mm) foam cushion on the back of the abrasive, with a cloth that grips on little T-spike protrusions from a hard pad. This is a very good system, and I am sure it will be popular.

Like everything else you attempt on a lathe, you have to develop skills when it comes to power abrading, and touch and sensitivity are required. With the lathe running anticlockwise, abrade from the centre outwards – that is, in an area between nine o'clock and seven o'clock of an imaginary clock face, or in the bottom half of the lathe's downward thrust, because this is the safest area. Avoid dwelling in the centre, or you will quickly abrade a depression. The full face of the disc is used only on flat surfaces. For curved surfaces, use the lower half of the disc. Let each grade of grit do its work before moving on to the next. You will develop other techniques, but these are the safest and best to start with.

I use a keyless chuck for speed. I have a number of pads lined in order with different grits of abrasive, and I peel the discs off only when they are worn to save time. The discs last longer, too. A belt cleaner (a solid latex-like block) is essential for removing dust and the build-up of resin from the discs, thus prolonging their life.

Depending on the diameter of your work, lathe speeds of 700–1400rpm are best; the larger the diameter, the slower the speed. Drill speeds are best between 2200 and 2800rpm. It is important that the lathe speed does not overpower the drill. For small work, a 400-watt drill will prove adequate; for larger work a 600-watt rating or higher is required, otherwise there is too much strain on the drill.

FINISHES

There are so many different finishes, with the various manufacturers making different and extravagant claims for each one, that we are spoilt for choice. However, if you analyse them, it becomes clear that most are basically very similar. Despite the different brand names, there are only three basic kinds: oil, wax and film barrier.

Oil finishes

Almost all my domestic pieces that will come in contact with food are finished with clear teak oil. This is very thin and penetrative. The oil is clear and of almost water-like consistency. It is based on mineral oil, but is much thinner. It is not a finish for display objects, and it is non-curing, so dust would be attracted. It is suitable for working objects, such as chopping boards, salad bowls and platters, and it is safe from the point of view of coming into contact with food. I suggest that objects are wiped clean after use with a damp sponge or cloth, while an occasional application of a vegetable oil will keep them looking fresh. Any surplus should be removed with a paper towel, and if the piece is burnished dry with a cloth, a warm patina will build up over the years.

Finishing in the lathe is as follows. After abrading through the required grits, stop the lathe and apply a liberal coat of oil with a soft cloth. Take some well-worn 320 grit (wet and dry paper or cloth-backed abrasive), restart the lathe and sand well into the wood. A slurry will be produced as you abrade to a silky satin finish. Apply another liberal coat of oil, take a handful of very soft shavings and burnish dry.

Another oil finish I use these days on a wide variety of work is Danish oil. It is not a quick finish but is reasonably easy to apply, although the build-up of sheen depends on the number of coats. This is a thin penetrating oil that

Using a handful of soft shavings to burnish the inside surface of a bowl to which a coat of oil has been applied

takes between four and eight hours to dry, depending on the conditions in the workshop. Application is best done with a piece of rag, while the lathe is stationary. Any surplus oil should be removed after a few minutes, and the piece is left to dry. When it is dry, dip an ultra-fine Scotch-Brite pad in the oil, which is used as a lubricant as you cut back the first dry coat with the lathe rotating. At this stage, I usually polish the object dry with a soft cloth – a satin finish should be the result.

You will now have a durable, moisture-resistant finish, which will be food-safe in three days, which is the time needed for total evaporation drying and the smell to disappear. If you like a higher gloss, repeat the process as many times as you like. It is possible to build up a glass-like surface, although I do not like high-gloss finishes, because I hate wood to look like plastic.

For safety, keep rags in a sealed jar or tin or lay them out flat. It is a good idea to destroy them after use whenever possible because spontaneous combustion is a real danger.

Wax finishes

At first sight, wax would seem to be the easiest of all finishes to apply, but it is not always the case. Most people think of beeswax, which is far too soft, or of carnauba, which is far too hard and gives a white, glassy shine.

Block wax

A 50/50 mixture of beeswax and carnauba, melted together with 10 per cent turpentine, makes a good block wax that you friction melt on your work. You can buy ready-prepared sticks from most polish suppliers, and this is the easiest thing to do.

If you want to make your own, put the waxes to be melted in a tin, and place this in a saucepan half-full of water. Melt gently, remove from the heat, stir in the turpentine and leave to solidify.

I used this kind of wax quite often in the past, usually applying it over a cut-back sealed surface. It is now some years since I used this system, as the advent of some superb soft-paste waxes has made it redundant.

Paste wax

I use soft-paste wax on bare wood and on wood that has been sealed. I apply wax to bare wood only in the finishing of my small boxes, which are made from very dense hardwoods on which sealers would just sit on the surface and not penetrate. Until 1993 I used a wax with a toluene constituent in it, a volatile substance with a smell I never liked, but it gave me the finish I wanted. Now I use a wax that has no toluene, which means that the finish is not quite so instantaneous, because the wax needs a little time to dry before polishing. It gives me a finish that is 95 per cent as good as the toluene-based wax on the day of making; but when it is left overnight, it is just as good. This wax is called Supreme and is made by Fiddes. I mentioned earlier that I use wax as a lubricant in finishing, and I have always abraded my boxes this way as it cuts down friction heat and dust, and, I believe, gives a better overall finish. When I used a toluene finishing wax, I abraded with another inert wax, but now I use Supreme wax for both abrading and finishing.

Any sealed surface needs to be cut back for whatever finish is to be applied. The Supreme wax mentioned above is compatible with both shellac- and lacquer-sealed surfaces, whereas toluene waxes are only compatible with lacquer.

Shellac-sealed finish

I used to use this kind of finish a great deal a few years ago, but new developments have rather overtaken it. I still prefer it to lacquer on timbers such as oak and elm, because it gives a softer, more natural, mellow look. After abrading is complete and with the lathe stationary, I apply a sparing coat of shellac sanding sealer with a mop brush. I allow it to dry – fifteen minutes is the absolute minimum drying time on items like bowls and dishes, but I much prefer to leave it overnight. Once it is dry, I cut back the excess sealer with the lathe rotating, using fine, well-worn abrasive dipped in wax or oil, depending on the finish I want. The wax or oil prevents the excess sealer from melting, whereas if it were sanded dry, rings of sealer, melted by friction heat, would appear round your work. After this process, use a fine Scotch-Brite pad, again dipped in wax or oil, to remove the last of the remaining excess sealer. You should now have a very silky smooth, sealer ring-free finish ready for the application of the final finish.

The sealer is used to fill the often coarse, open pores that are seen on timbers like oak and elm. Left untreated, the surface would soon attract dust and grime and quickly look dirty.

If you use oil over the sealed finish, apply it with a soft cloth while the lathe is stationary, then start the lathe and friction burnish dry with a soft cloth or shavings. If you opt for a polish finish, use a soft-paste wax rather than block wax.

If you used a burr wood (see page 37), there are often little bud-eye growth holes that the wax will fill. Use an old toothbrush to remove this while the wax is still soft. If you do not, the wax will dry in the holes and spoil the effect because it will usually be a different colour from the wood.

Cellulose lacquer

I tend to use this kind of finish on items made from white or light timbers and from dark woods, like ebony, when the object is designed to be purely decorative. My choice is a thin, pre-cat satin lacquer. This is applied after abrading, quickly with a mop brush while the lathe is stationary. Try not to cause a build-up of lacquer by going over the same surface twice during this application. Unless the item being finished is very small, it is best if you leave the piece to dry for twelve to eighteen hours after application. With very fine abrasive, 400 or 500 grit, dipped in soft-paste wax and with the lathe rotating, cut back any surplus sealer. Follow this with a wax-free ultra-fine Scotch-Brite pad. You should now have a very smooth, sealed surface, free from sealer ring build-up and ready for final finishing.

You could now apply another thin coat of lacquer and repeat the process outlined above, which will give a heavier lacquer finish that is more moisture-resistant. Unless the wood has very open pores, I generally apply just one coat of lacquer and, having carried out the process described, I apply soft-paste wax (usually Supreme wax) with the lathe stationary. I let this dry and polish with a soft cloth with the lathe rotating. This finish will normally stop the white fingerprint bloom that people with clammy hands can impart to objects that do not have a true moisture-proof finish. Additional coats of lacquer build up a better moisture resistance, but the wood does not look so natural.

You will note there has been no mention of instant-shine polishes, polyurethane, two-part mixes and so on. This is because I dislike finishes that give a high gloss or skin-like barrier to the wood's surface. These products have their place, but I prefer not to use them on my work. I think that a high gloss makes wood look cheap and plastic-like, and a heavy build-up of polish seems to block the natural beauty of the wood and remove its wonderful tactile quality. If, by chance, I obtain a high gloss finish on my work, I cut this back to a satin sheen.

SHAPE AND FORM

Purity of form, life and lift are the characteristics I look for in most objects. I do not like heavy ornamentation or the imposition of craftsmanship for its own sake. Good, fluid, elegant design does not need the addition of features that interrupt the visual enjoyment of pure form. I am not suggesting that there should be no embellishment or refined detail, for these have an important part to play in any design process, but the overuse of these elements adds clutter and breaks up continuity. I have always believed that there should be a good reason for adding any decoration, and I usually reserve it for linking a change of surface direction, giving a focal point in a boring material, balancing a proportion or finishing a rim or base.

It is difficult to create completely new shapes and forms. Innovation lies in developing, manipulating, refining and redesigning – rather like reinventing the wheel. One change that has occurred in recent years is that many shapes, which formerly had seemed to be the province only of the potter and the metalworker, have entered the vocabulary of the woodturner.

I have never studied form in the sense that I pored over books or visited a great number of museums, but I have always been interested in design and have more than twenty books on the subject. I am also aware of the fact that most pleasing vessel and bowl forms have evolved over many centuries and from many cultures of the world. I have learned about shape and form mainly by observing, but I have never wanted to get so close that I could be unduly influenced by any one style or culture. I admire both the classic designs of the past and many more contemporary designs, with their origins in cultures as diverse as Egyptian, Greek, Chinese, Japanese, African, South America Indian and North American Pueblo Indian. This is a rich and diverse list, but the overriding reason for the appeal in each case is their elegance and purity.

DESIGNING DOMESTIC WARES

The making of things for use around the home holds great appeal, and I am sure that often the promise of such wares forms the prelude of justification for the first purchase of a lathe to a doubting partner. My own turning career began in this area, and even today 50 per cent of my income comes from making such pieces. Objects for every room in the home can be made on a lathe, from light pulls to curtain rings, from balustrades to porch posts, from candle holders to standard lamps, from salt bowls to salad bowls... the list is almost endless.

I have always concentrated on items for the kitchen and table, although there is, inevitably, some overlap about where and how individual pieces are used. In each area, before you begin to make anything, there are a number of things to consider, ranging from timber choice to design.

Kitchen and table ware

Items for use in the kitchen have been made for centuries, and a well-proven formula that takes into account both their function and the materials from which they are best made has evolved over the years. We would not be human if we were not always looking for ways to improve things, but change for its own sake should be avoided unless it creates something that does a job as well or better. It is possible to make subtle design changes that make an object fresh and modern without undermining its proven function.

Many utensils for use in the kitchen are available very cheaply in the shops. Most of these are mass-produced and imported, and if you intend to produce work to sell wholesale do not try to compete in this market, unless you like volume repetitiveness with a small profit. Specialist kitchen/cookware shops exist, however, and these are always looking out for quality, individual products, for which they are prepared to pay a realistic price.

The production of items for the table is an area that affords opportunities to produce a wide range of pieces that can give great pleasure in use if they are well designed and made correctly. It is possible to make an item that looks pleasing but is useless for its intended purpose; it is also possible to make an item that looks dreadful but performs the function for which it was intended. Neither result is acceptable: your aim should be to produce something that functions well and is aesthetically pleasing.

Design

A minimalist approach is best. Keep your design simple and uncluttered, avoiding fussy patterns that will create food traps and make things difficult to clean. Remember that most items are functional. A bowl that holds granules should not tip or spill easily; tall items should not be unbalanced; an egg cup should hold an egg properly, with a correct interior depth and diameter. You must take the use into account in all your designs. As I noted earlier, I love pure form. I do not like busy, fussy ornamentation, much preferring minimal, refined, detailed embellishment.

Materials

Traditionally, sycamore, maple, beech, hornbeam and fruitwoods have been used, with some small items being made from boxwood and holly. It is no accident that these woods have become very popular with many turners. Although they are mostly fairly bland in appearance, they are close-grained, work well, are stable in use and almost odourless, which is very important as they will not impart any taint or smell to food.

Finishes

After use, kitchen ware should be washed and scrubbed clean under a running tap. Do not use polishes on such items, because these can impart taint and smell. Any finish

Classic footed bowl made from
pink ivory wood

applied should be oil, and my preference is for thin mineral oil, which is clear and does not discolour the wood. If you prefer, you can use walnut, sunflower, corn or any vegetable oil. Olive oil is rather sticky, however, and is far from ideal.

Materials and marketing

If you are making things for your own use or in small quantities for direct sale, you can use almost any material you wish, from plain to flamboyantly figured, as long as it is suitable for the purpose. However, if you supply shops on a regular wholesale basis, as I do, you will have to be more selective in what you offer. This is a competitive world, so you should select timbers that work well, that can be obtained without difficulty on a regular, ongoing basis. Larger-scale work should be offered only in a limited range of timbers, although small items can be supplied in a wider range.

The public seems to have a preconceived idea of the kind of prices they are prepared to pay for functional work, unless it is made in some exceptionally figured wood, so efficient making and prudent buying of materials are called for. I have always aimed to make work of a high standard, to sell at the middle and top end of the market. I am at a loss to know why so many people still produce poor quality work by hand. The difference in time to make something well or poorly is often quite small, and surely one of the reasons for making something by hand is to produce an object that is better than a similar object made on a machine. In addition, what satisfaction is there in making something of poor quality?

Burr myrtle wood bowl, left natural on the underside and with an inset foot, turned smooth on the top

Six-piece Indian ebony pagoda box with chatter work on the lid

THE PROJECTS

This range of domestic wares for use in the kitchen and dining room utilizes simple design with the emphasis being on pure form. The items are intended for everyday use, so they have been made with a view to avoiding food traps and facilitating easy cleaning. They incorporate no heavy detail – a minimalist approach has been adopted.

Ash salad bowls

CHOPPING BOARD

The progression of a chopping board, from bark-edged plank to circular blank to finished piece

Keep the design simple and practical, avoiding deep grooves, undercut shoulders and so on, so that you do not create traps for food or make a board that is difficult to clean.

SUGGESTED LATHE TOOLS

Screw chuck
½in (12mm) bowl gouge
1¼in (31mm) square-ended scraper
½in (12mm) spindle gouge (modified)
1½in (38mm) Key shear scraper (optional)

Timber

A disc of 1½in (38mm) dry sycamore, quarter-sawn to minimize distortion, is ideal. If this is not available, choose well-seasoned wood – I use kiln-dried timber – that has not been fast grown. Check the spacing of the growth rings, remembering that the more widely spaced they are, the softer and faster grown the timber. Select a close-grained wood, which will absorb less moisture, distort less and stand up to constant knife cuts.

Size

I suggest that the board be between 9in (230mm) and 16in (405mm) in diameter. I turn any size within this range

Fig 32a Fast-grown quarter-sawn section

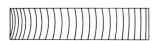

Fig 32b Slow-grown quarter-sawn section – the ideal

Fig 33a Fast-grown through-sawn section – prone to distortion

Fig 33b Slow-grown through-sawn, best used in this manner – if it distorts, it will not rock in use

on a screw chuck with a diameter of 4–5in (100–125mm). A screw chuck will leave you with only one hole to fill in the base, rather than the two or three that will result if you use a faceplate. Other mounting methods could be used – glue joints, for example – but these are slow and messy.

Preparing the base

Unless you friction-grip the disc in some way, you will need to prepare the base before mounting it on the lathe or you will not be able to turn it. If you have a planer or some form of large sander, it is easy to obtain a flat surface. I have a 15in (380mm) thicknesser, but failing this, hand-plane or power-plane the base of the board true and flat across the grain and sand to finish.

Chucking and turning

Drill a pilot hole, ⅝in (16mm) deep, in the centre of the base with a ¼in (6mm) diameter countersink drill. Mount the disc on the screw chuck. Use a lathe speed of around 800rpm, making sure the disc is clear of the tool rest, and true up the outside diameter with a sharp, high-speed, ½in (12mm), steel bowl gouge.

Truing up the face

Move the rest parallel to the face, but slightly below centre. Using the same gouge, start to true the face, working from the middle outwards. (There will be no need to do this if you have a surface thicknesser.) Hold the gouge blade between your left index finger and thumb and pull the gouge along the tool rest with your left hand, pushing the handle with your right hand. This will produce a traversing effect that should enable you to achieve a true face with few undulations or ripples.

Final face tooling

Remove any surface ripples with a high-speed, 1¼in (31mm), square-ended, steel scraper. Set the tool rest parallel to the face at, or slightly above, centre height, so that the scraper tilts downwards by 10–15 per cent, to cut on the top-edge burr from the grinder. Again, allow your index finger to be in contact with the tool rest, so that sideways traversing movements, guided by your finger, produce a true surface.

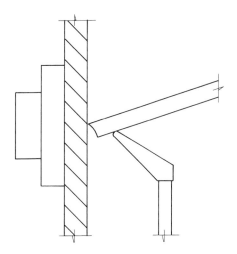

Fig 34 Final face tooling with the scraper tilted downwards

Shaping the corners

Next shape the hard square corners. For this you need a ½in (12mm) spindle gouge, fingernail-shaped but with a bowl gouge ground angle. Move the tool rest back to the edge and pull the gouge forwards from both the top and bottom faces towards the centre of the edge, in order to

Shaping the edges with a ½in
(12mm) spindle gouge

Final finish – shaping the edges
with a Key shear scraper

create a soft radius. Cut only in the first ⅜in (9mm) or so
near the tip of the gouge. With the tool handle held well
down, you should make shearing cuts with bevel support
to leave a clean surface. If you have one, you may find
that a Key shear scraper blends surfaces together better.

Sanding

The board is now ready for sanding. I power-sand with 3in
(75mm) Velcro-backed discs of 120, 180 and 240 grit
abrasives, but use whatever method you prefer.

Finishing

With the lathe stationary, apply a liberal coat of clear teak
mineral oil. Then, with the lathe switched on, sand this well
in with worn 320 grit, aluminium oxide, flexible wet and dry
paper. Apply a further coat of oil and, with the lathe
rotating, burnish with fine finishing cut shavings. Remove
the board from the chuck and fill the screw hole with plastic
wood or a wooden plug. Leave the filler or glue to dry
overnight before sanding and finishing the base. I use an
orbital palm sander for finishing prior to oiling.

Completed chopping boards in two different diameters (9in/230mm and 12in/305mm)

PESTLE AND
MORTAR

The mortar blank is shown here drilled ready for mounting on a pin chuck and then with the outside shaped

Design

The mortar bowl is different from almost any other sort of bowl you might make because it is used for pounding and grinding herbs and spices. It must, therefore, be made from a much heavier section than normal. As with anything that is going to contain powder or small granules, it is best if the bowl has in-curved or, at least, straight sides; it should certainly not be openly dished or flared. The pestle needs to be rather chunky to give weight for pounding The bowl is designed to be held against the body as you pound your herbs.

Timber

The articles illustrated were made from a 5 x 3in (125 x 75mm) disc (for the mortar) and a 6 x 1$\frac{1}{2}$ x 1$\frac{1}{2}$in (150 x 38 x 38mm) block (for the pestle).

The alternative mortar, which is shown on page 68, is end-grain turned and needs a piece 6 x 4 x 4in (150 x 100 x 100mm); it is made in a different way, although the pestle is made from the same material and in the same way as the main pestle.

Ash is a good choice for this project, but you can use any timber as long as it does not have a strong scent that could taint the herbs and spices.

MORTAR

SUGGESTED LATHE TOOLS

1in (25mm) pin chuck

$^3/_8$in (9mm) screw chuck

$^1/_2$in (12mm) or $^3/_8$in (9mm) bowl gouge

1$^1/_4$in (31mm) square-ended scraper

1$^1/_2$in (38mm) Key shear scraper (optional)

1$^1/_2$in (38mm) Key French curve scraper (optional)

$^1/_2$in (12mm) diamond-point scraper (optional)

Chucking and turning the outside

Use a spade, Forstner or saw-tooth bit to drill a 1in (25mm) hole in the centre of the mortar disc, stopping $^7/_8$in (22mm) short of the base. Mount your disc on a 1in (25mm) pin chuck – expanding ones are best – and select a lathe speed of 1200–1500rpm.

Shape the outside of the bowl with a $^1/_2$in (12mm) bowl gouge, cutting from the base towards the top with easy, fluid movements. Aim for the maximum diameter of the bowl to be at a distance of about $^5/_8$in (15–16mm) from the top, with the top itself slightly in-curved. The base should be about 1$^1/_2$–1$^5/_8$in (38–41mm) across. You should find that you are able to create smooth curves within these parameters. Final finishing cuts are best taken with a 1$^1/_2$in (38mm) Key shear scraper, but a 1$^1/_4$in (31mm) square-ended scraper works almost as well.

Incise two little V-grooves near the top with a diamond-point scraper as decoration.

Shaping the outside of the mortar with a $^1/_2$in (12mm) bowl gouge

Base and drilling

The base needs to be tooled so that it is slightly concave. For screw-chuck mounting, a pilot hole, some $^1/_2$in (12mm) deep and $^1/_4$in (6mm) in diameter, is required in the centre of the bowl. This can be made by using the tailstock with a Jacob's chuck and drill. An alternative and quicker method, but one that requires a certain amount of practice, is to use the drill hand-held in a chuck. A countersink recess is formed with the point of a skew chisel: the tool rest supports the drill while an accurate hole is drilled by pushing the drill to the required depth into the rotating bowl. You may find it helps to wind some masking tape around the drill as a depth guide.

Drilling a pilot hole in the centre of the mortar base in preparation for screw-chuck mounting

Sanding

The outside of the mortar is now ready for sanding. You could power-sand it with 3in (75mm) Velcro-backed discs of 120, 180 and 240 grit abrasives, or use your own preferred method.

Finishing

Apply a liberal coat of clear teak mineral oil and sand well in with worn, 320 grit, aluminium oxide, flexible wet and dry abrasive paper. Use fine finishing shavings to burnish dry a second coat of oil, then remove the mortar bowl from the pin chuck.

Hollowing the mortar with a ½in
(12mm) bowl gouge

Hollowing the mortar

Mount the mortar bowl on a ⅜in (9mm) parallel screw
chuck – this is the reason the ¼in (6mm) pilot hole was
drilled. True the top of the bowl with a ½in (12mm) bowl
gouge, then begin to hollow, using either a ½in (12mm)
or a ⅜in (9mm) bowl gouge. Your aim is to make cuts that
progressively open out and deepen the bowl. Make
sweeping movements that cut towards the bottom, starting
from the top of the 1in (25mm) drill hole. Throughout the
process, the flute of the gouge should be presented at an
angle of 45 degrees out of the vertical, with its bevel
rubbing in support of the cut. The drill spur mark will give
you an automatic depth stop. With practice, you will be
able to complete the tooling with the gouge. However, most
people will find it helpful to use a shaped, French curve
scraper to remove the ripples made by the gouge.

Sanding and finishing

Repeat the sanding and finishing methods described
previously for the outside of the bowl, but a 2in (50mm)
Velcro-backed disc will be better inside the bowl. Finally,
remove from the screw chuck, fill or plug the hole and,
when dry, finish off.

Alternative mortar design in ash

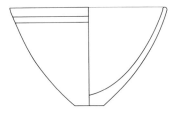 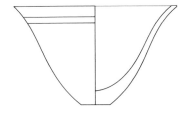 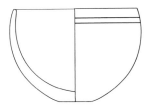

Fig 35 Open bowl, weak in form for its purpose   **Fig 36** A worse example than Fig 35   **Fig 37** A proven design

Finished pestle and mortar made in ash

The development of the pestle from rectangular blank to near completion

PESTLE

SUGGESTED LATHE TOOLS

¾in (18mm) roughing gouge
¾in (18mm) skew chisel
⅜in (9mm) spindle gouge
⅜in (9mm) beading tool

Turning

Mount the 6 x 1½ x 1½in (150 x 38 x 38mm) piece between centres and rough out the shape of the pestle with a ¾in (18mm) roughing gouge. For ease of turning, it will be best if the bulbous end is towards the headstock. The main body shape is refined with a ¾in

(18mm) skew chisel, while detailed work round the holding end should be done with a ⅜in (9mm) spindle gouge and a ⅜in (9mm) beading tool. The two V-grooves in the pestle stem, which repeat the design around the mortar, can be cut either with the point of the skew chisel or with the beading tool.

Shaping the main body of the pestle with a ¾in (18mm) skew chisel

.Cutting the V-grooves in the stem of the pestle with the point of the skew chisel

Sanding and finishing

Hand-sand in the lathe with 150, 180 and 240 grit, aluminium oxide, flexible wet and dry paper, apply clear teak mineral oil and sand again with worn 320 grit abrasive of the same type. Friction dry with a polishing cloth. Remove from the lathe and cut off the surplus material at each end before buff-sanding on a foam drum sander. Finally, oil and hand-sand.

The completed pestle and mortar (centre) with the sugar bowl (left) and salt
bowl (right) giving an idea of size and form

SALT AND SUGAR BOWLS

Salt bowl blank ready for turning and with the first roughing out
stage completed

Design

Both these projects serve similar functions in that they are
intended to hold granules, and the design must take the use
into account. In-curved and straight-sided designs, similar to
those shown in Figs 40 and 41, are best, while Fig 42
illustrates the kind of shape to avoid (see page 74). Stability
is also important, and a height that is between two-fifths and
two-thirds of the base is advocated, a proportion that still
gives the opportunity to produce pleasing shapes. Bowls with
smaller bases can be made (see pages 110–117), but these
would not be suitable for sugar or salt because they will be
inherently unstable and could easily be tipped over. Such
bowls are of a more decorative nature.

SALT BOWL

SUGGESTED LATHE TOOLS

Drive centres
Contracting jaw chuck
¾in (18mm) skew chisel
⅜in (9mm) Key gouge (or modify your own)
⅛in (3mm) parting tool
¾–1in (18–25mm) round-ended scraper
⅜in (9mm) spindle gouge
¾in (18mm) straight chisel (optional)
⅜in (9mm) beading/parting tool (optional)

Timber

The bowls are best made in pairs from end-grained wood, and a piece 3½ x 3½ x 2in (90 x 90 x 50mm) is ideal. Yew was used for the salt bowl shown here.

Preparatory turning

Mount the block between centres and turn to create a cylinder, using a roughing gouge. Square each end with a parting tool or the point of a skew chisel, with the lathe speed set to 1300–1800rpm. The best way to hold the cylinder to make the bowls is in a contracting dovetail jaw chuck. You need to cut a short undercut tenon/spigot on one end that is compatible with the chuck jaw size you select. I used an Axminster precision four-jaw with 1½in (38mm) O'Donnell dovetail spigot jaws. Once you have cut the tenon/spigot, you can remove the cylinder from the lathe together with the drive centres. On many lathes it is best if the tailstock is also removed at this stage.

Chucking and truing the outside

Mount your selected contraction dovetail-type chuck in the lathe and tighten the jaws on the tenon/spigot on your prepared cylinder. True up the cylinder with either a ¾in (18mm) skew chisel or a ¾in (18mm) straight-across chisel. This is best done with the rest set quite high, and if you imagine the end of your cylinder to be a clock face, your chisel should be cutting as if the hour hand were at 10.30. You can true the cylinder with either the point or the heel of the skew chisel leading, but whichever method you use, cutting should take place in the tool's lower section and certainly not above its centre.

Your grip on the tool is important. Ideally, your index finger is below the chisel and in contact with the rest, acting as a guide for the traversing cuts that are to be made. Your thumb is on top of the tool, applying a light, even pressure both downwards and sideways. This position keeps the tool in contact with the rest and helps to control the traversing movements. Make light cuts either towards the head- or tailstock ends of the lathe, which should produce fine shavings and a smooth, true cylinder. True the end of what will be the top of the first bowl with the point of a skew chisel.

Marking out

Set a pair of dividers to 1⅜in (35mm). With the lathe running, and supporting the dividers on the tool rest, use one of the divider points to mark the length of the first bowl, rubbing the other leg on the top of the bowl. Leave a gap of about ⅛in (3mm) and mark the length of the second bowl with both divider points.

Outside shaping

Use a ⅛in (3mm) parting tool to make a channel about ⅝in (15–16mm) deep between the two bowls. Start to shape the radius near the bowl base with a spindle gouge, a beading tool or the point of a skew chisel. Once you have achieved the shape you require, cut two V-grooves near the top of the bowl with the point of the skew chisel. You can shape the outside of both the bowls at this stage if you wish.

Shaping with a ⅜in (9mm) beading/parting tool

Inside hollowing

Position the tool rest across the top of the first bowl, just below its centre height. Take a ⅜in (9mm) Key high-speed steel spindle gouge. This is a heavily modified tool with many uses, and its tip has a 60–65 degree angle instead of the normal 30 degrees. Present the gouge to the centre of the bowl on its edge, with the open face of the flute towards you, holding it horizontal and parallel to the bed. Tilt the gouge face away from you so that it is 10–15 degrees out of the vertical. Now push the gouge towards the headstock. You will find that it acts just like a drill. Set a depth gauge to leave about 3/16in (4mm) in the base of the bowl.

Open up the bowl by making pivoting, scooping cuts with the gouge flute, which should now be tilted away from you, some 45 degrees out of the vertical. These cuts deepen and open up the bowl, with the bevel rubbing most of the time. You can remove 95–98 per cent of the bowl's interior in this way. Use a rounded shape scraper to clean up any ripples, working from the base outwards and drawing the scraper up the side wall towards you. Aim to have the final wall about ⅛in (3mm) thick.

Note that these methods of hollowing are used only for objects made from end-grain material.

Clear teak mineral oil is applied then friction dried with a cloth

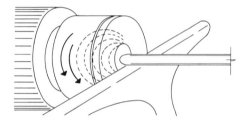

Fig 38 The start of the hollowing process

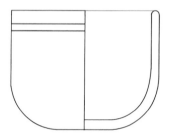

Fig 40 Ideal shape for salt or sugar

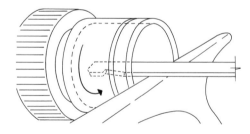

Fig 39 Final scraping of the inside

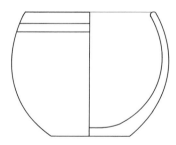

Fig 41 Another ideal shape for salt or sugar

Sanding, oiling and parting

Hand-sand with 150, 180 and 240 grit, aluminium oxide, flexible wet and dry paper, then apply clear teak mineral oil or your own preferred finish. Sand again with worn 320 grit abrasive of the same type and friction dry with a polishing cloth.

Part off the first bowl with a ⅛in (3mm) parting tool. You can now make the second bowl in exactly the same way.

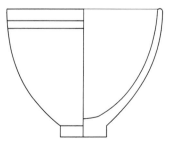

Fig 42 Easily tipped in use

Finishing the base

The base needs to be finished so that it is smooth, and this can be done in several ways. The simplest methods are to sand by rubbing the piece on abrasive placed on a flat surface or to use a disc or pad in a drilling machine. However, the most professional way is to reverse-chuck the bowl. Most people will find it easiest to use a wooden friction jam chuck. Either cut a spigot, onto which you can push the bowl – make sure that you do not force the fit or it could split – or cut a recess into which you can push it. The shape of the bowl will dictate which method you adopt. Neither the spigot nor the recess needs to be more than ¼in (6mm) long or deep. If you have the option, wooden four-jaw plates on a contracting and expanding chuck will be quicker. Once the piece is mounted, take very light cuts with a sharp, ⅜in (9mm) spindle gouge to make the base slightly concave. Sand and polish the salt bowl to finish the item.

Finished salt bowl and scoop made in yew

SUGAR BOWL

SUGGESTED LATHE TOOLS

Pin chuck
Contracting/expanding jaw chuck
3⁄8–1⁄2in (9–12mm) bowl gouges
1–1 1⁄2in (25–38mm) square-ended scraper
or 1 1⁄2in (38mm) Key shear scraper
1⁄8in (3mm) parting tool
1⁄2in (12mm) diamond-point scraper
1 1⁄4in (31mm) curved scraper
3⁄8in (9mm) spindle gouge (modified)

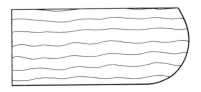

Fig 43 Cross-grained timber section

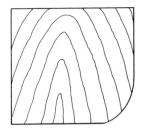

Fig 44 End-grained timber section

Timber

Cross-grained cherry wood was selected for this project. The following principles should govern the choice of grain direction for objects: if the diameter is greater than the height, use cross-grain timber; if the diameter is smaller than the height, use end-grain timber. Exceptions include small items like the salt bowl or special-effect pieces.

Size

The suggested dimensions for the sugar bowl are a diameter of 4in (100mm) by a depth of 2in (50mm) or a diameter of 5in (125mm) by a depth of 2 1⁄2in (64mm). The bowl illustrated is the smaller size.

Development of the sugar bowl

Preparation for turning

Mark out and cut a 4in (100mm) disc on the band saw. Drill a 1in (25mm) hole with a spade, Forstner or saw-tooth bit in the centre, stopping ⁵⁄₁₆in (7–8mm) short of the base. This will act as a depth stop when you are hollowing.

Chucking and turning the outside

Mount the piece on a 1in (25mm) pin chuck – expanding ones are best – and select a lathe speed of 1200–1500rpm. Start to shape the outside of the bowl, cutting from the base to the top with a ½in (12mm), high-speed, steel bowl gouge. This is best used with the flute towards you and held at an angle of about 45 degrees out of the vertical. The gouge bevel supports the cut, rubbing just behind the cutting edge. The base should be made

Shaping the outside of the bowl with a ½in (12mm) bowl gouge

Continue to shape the surface after forming a recess in the base to accommodate your chosen chuck

slightly concave so that the bowl will be stable. To give the best finish, the final shaping of the surface should be done with either a 1–1½in (25–38mm) square-ended scraper or a 1½in (38mm) Key shear scraper.

A small recess needs to be cut at this stage to accommodate your chosen chuck. I used a 1½in (38mm) expansion on this occasion. Set a pair of dividers to your required dimension and mark this diameter on the base. Use a ⅛in (3mm) parting tool to cut a recess to a maximum depth of ⅛in (3mm). The recess should be slightly undercut to allow the dovetail action of the chuck jaws to grip with maximum effect. Complete the tooling by incising two V-grooves near the top of the bowl with a small diamond-point scraper.

Sanding

The outside of the bowl is now ready for sanding. Power-sand with 2in (50mm) or 3in (75mm) Velcro-backed discs of 120, 180 and 240 grit or use your preferred method.

Finishing

Apply a liberal coat of clear teak mineral oil and sand well in with worn 320 grit, aluminium oxide, flexible wet and dry abrasive. Another coat of oil is burnished dry with fine shavings or cloth. Remove the piece from the pin chuck.

Hollowing the bowl

The method described here should be used for hollowing out all cross-grained objects. It is the opposite of the method used for end-grain turning.

True the bowl top with a ⅜in (9mm) high-speed steel bowl gouge. Hollow out the bowl, using the same gouge to make opening and deepening cuts with sweeping movements towards the bottom, starting from the top of the 1in (25mm) hole. The gouge is used with the flute tilted away from you and held at an angle of 45 degrees out of the vertical. As the bowl gets thinner, you will find it helpful if the four fingers of the left hand cup the outside of the bowl, with only the thumb in contact with the gouge, to steady and guide it. The fingers will absorb any vibration or flexing of the bowl.

Once the wall is about $\frac{3}{16}$in (4–5mm) thick, lightly skim the surface with a suitably shaped scraper. Depending on the shape, you may need two scrapers to blend the curves. But you should find that most of the shapes you create can be tooled to conclusion with a sharp French curve scraper. It is best to make light skimming and pushing cuts from the top of the bowl towards the bottom to remove any ripples that have been caused by the gouge. Never exert pressure on the side of the bowl by pushing outwards or by pulling the tool from the centre against it. Both methods can induce chatter and cause the grain to tear and, in extreme cases, can crack or even shatter thin-walled bowls. When you use the scraper, cup the bowl with your fingers and allow your thumb to rest on top of the tool. Remember that the gouge should do 95 to 98 per cent of the tooling, so that use of the scraper is kept to a minimum.

Sanding and finishing

Repeat the procedure outlined on page 77 for the outside of the bowl, although you will find that 2in (50mm) Velcro-backed discs are the largest size that can be used. Remove the bowl ready for finishing the base.

Finishing the base

I do not like chuck-holding marks to be visible on items like this, so reverse-chucking is necessary, and the methods suggested for the salt bowl should be used here. Use either a wooden friction jam chuck or four jaw plates mounted on a contraction/expansion chuck to hold the bowl. The chuck marks are best removed with a $\frac{3}{8}$in (9mm) spindle gouge with a fingernail shape, ground with an acute angle – 55–65 degrees works well. The intention is not to remove the entire recess but to get rid of the hard dovetail undercut by creating a soft, flowing curve. Once this is achieved, hand-sand and oil to finish.

Finished sugar bowl and scoop made in cherry

SUGAR AND SALT SPOONS

These designs combine a spoon-like handle with a scoop-like bowl. As both are similar in concept, with size being the only difference, their making is described together.

The overall finished lengths of the sugar and salt spoons should be 4½in (115mm) and 2½in (64mm), respectively. The whole process, from selecting your wood to the finished product, should take less than ten minutes.

SUGGESTED LATHE TOOLS

Sugar spoon

Four-prong drive centre

Revolving cone centre

⅜in (9mm) spindle gouge

¾in (18mm) skew chisel

⅛in (3mm) parting tool

Salt spoon

As above but a ½in (12mm) skew or ⅜in (9mm) parting tool is better than a ¾in (18mm) skew

---

Fig 45 Normal scoop

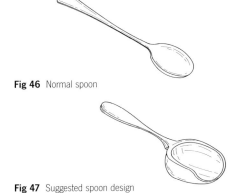

Fig 46 Normal spoon

Fig 47 Suggested spoon design

Preparation and timber

The methods described for making these items may not be possible if you do not possess a router, so an alternative method is outlined on page 81.

The timber for the sugar spoon should be straight and close-grained, 5 x 1¼ x 1¼in (125 x 31 x 31mm); for the salt spoon use a piece 6 x ½ x ½in (150 x 12 x 12mm), which will make two spoons. The inside of the scoop-like end is created by pushing the square ends down on top of a round-nosed cutter. The router is set up as if it were to be used as a spindle moulder. Clamp or screw to the router fence a wooden jig that will admit the 1¼in (31mm) square for the sugar spoon, and another that will admit the ½in (12mm) square should be made for the salt spoon. These jigs are set centrally over the cutter, making it possible to produce an even wall thickness.

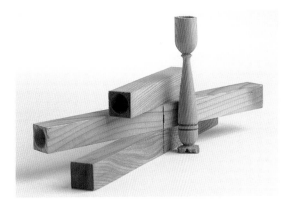

Salt scoop blank marked out, showing routed end, and with shaping complete

Sugar scoop blank marked out, showing routed end, and with shaping complete

Using a router

With the router switched off, push the 1¼in (31mm) square into the jig hole until it rests on top of the cutter. Use a pencil to mark a line on the square that is level with the jig top. Remove and make a second mark 1⅜in (34mm) from the first. This second mark is your stop line when you push down on the router cutter, and it can be used to mark out as many squares as you have prepared so that there is a uniform depth in all of them.

The aim is to produce a square with a 1⅜in (34mm) deep, domed hole, 1in (25mm) in diameter, by using a 1in (25mm) round-nosed cutter. This size has been carefully worked out so that, after all the shaping has been done, the spoon will hold a measure of sugar similar to a normal heaped teaspoon. It will be easier if you use a smaller cutter – a ¾in (18mm), for example – before the 1in (25mm) tool, because this greatly reduces the resistance that would be met if you were to push straight down on to a large cutter. Carbide-tipped cutters are best, but a high-speed one will do.

Pushing the end of the sugar scoop blank on to a router cutter

Whichever kind you use, keep them sharp. This may sound a long and complicated process, but once you have jigged up the router, it takes only a few seconds to produce the domed hole.

The domed hole in the salt spoon is made in an identical way, except that the cutter is smaller – ⅜in (9mm) in diameter – and the hole is ⅝in (15mm) deep. Create two spoons from the 6in (150mm) piece, pushing each end down on to the cutter in the ½in (12mm) square jig. The squares you push into both jigs should be a good fit, because any looseness will cause cutter chatter and a ragged surface.

Fig 48 Sugar spoon blank after routing

Fig 49 Salt spoons after routing both ends of blank

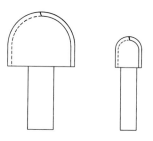

Fig 50 Domed router cutters

Cut the salt spoons into two 3in (75mm) lengths, then use the band saw to cut a cross, about ⅛in (3mm) deep, on each solid end and the solid end of the sugar spoon. The four-prong drive centre will locate in these crosses.

Using a lathe

Mount a small four-prong drive centre in the headstock and a revolving cone centre in the tailstock. Mount the sugar scoop square between these centres, taking care not to exert undue pressure as this could split the scoop. With the lathe set to 1300–1500rpm, reduce your square into a cylinder with a ⅜in (9mm) spindle gouge or a ¾in (18mm) skew chisel. Set a pair of dividers to about 1⁹⁄₁₆in (40mm) and mark a line from the tailstock end. Use a ⅛in (3mm) parting tool on this line until the diameter is ½in (12mm).

Reduce the handle size with the gouge, shaping this and the spoon bowl profile close to your desired shape. The final shaping of the handle and spoon bowl is done with the ¾in (18mm) skew chisel, which I like to use with the point leading. Continue the decorative theme by cutting two V-grooves near the top of the handle with the skew point.

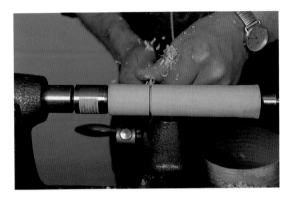

Using a parting tool to define the sugar scoop from the handle

Shaping the spoon end of the sugar scoop on a disc sander

Shaping the section between the sugar scoop and the handle with a skew chisel

centre, creating a morse-taper effect. Go right through, so you can use a knock-out bar to remove waste material. Spoon blanks have a taper turned on them between centres, compatible with that in your wooden chuck. Tap this into your chuck with a mallet, centring it as true as possible. Turn the projecting spoon blank true. Hollow out the spoon end in the same way as was described for making a salt bowl. Turning the spoon head and handle can normally be done by supporting the whole thing with the fingers of the left hand, but if this proves difficult, bring up the tailstock with a revolving cone centre for support. The rest of the making procedure is as described already.

Sanding and finishing

Sand by hand with the lathe speed to the same setting as the one at which you turned the spoon. Use 150, 180 and 240 grit, aluminium oxide, flexible wet and dry abrasive paper. Apply a liberal coat of oil and sand it in with worn 320 grit paper. Oil again and polish dry.

Remove from the lathe and cut off the waste material from the handle end. A drum or disc/belt sander is very useful for making items like this. Shape the spoon end as required, hand-sand the handle and spoon ends and finish with oil.

Cup chuck method

If you use this method, the spoon blanks need to be larger – 6 x 1½ x 1½in (150 x 38 x 38mm) for the sugar spoon and 4 x ⅝ x ⅝in (100 x 15 x 15mm) for each salt spoon.

Mount a wooden disc on a faceplate or turn one to fit inside a metal cup chuck, and turn a tapered hole in the

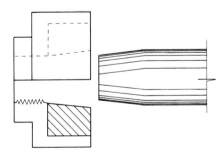

Fig 51 Cup chuck with a tapered wooden inset plus the tapered spoon blank

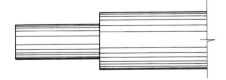

Fig 52 Blank prepared for collet or Jacob's chuck

P E P P E R   M I L L

Pepper mill blank; the blank shaped into a cylinder; the shaping of the base completed

A lot of pepper mills are not well designed. They often look, and actually are, unbalanced because the diameter at the base is too small in relation to the height, which also makes it difficult to create good form (see Figs 57a and b and 58a and b which illustrate this point). Even when the diameter is large enough, the shaping often starts too near the base, again making the finished mill look unbalanced. Good design is a question of balanced proportion, and an important principle to bear in mind is that no part of the design should be greater in diameter than that near the base area. This will considerably increase your chances of success. Here are some guide sizes:

6 x 2⅛ x 2⅛in (152 x 54 x 54mm)
8 x 2¼ x 2¼in (203 x 57 x 57mm)
10 x 2⅜ x 2⅜in (254 x 60 x 60mm)
12 x 2½ x 2½in (304 x 64 x 64mm)

A diameter less than this will make the job of creating a balanced design very difficult and greatly reduce the stability of the finished piece. It is worth noting that the wooden area normally finishes ⅜–½in (9–12mm) shorter than the stated mill size because this includes the knob. This should produce a well-balanced mill that not only looks good but feels good in the hand. Remember that soft, rounded shapes are always more pleasurable to use than hard, lined forms.

SUGGESTED LATHE TOOLS

Four-prong drive centre

Cone revolving centre

Contracting spigot chuck

$\frac{3}{4}$in (18mm) roughing gouge

$\frac{1}{8}$in (3mm) parting tool

$\frac{3}{8}$in (9mm) parting/beading tool

$\frac{3}{4}$in (18mm) skew chisel

$\frac{3}{8}$–$\frac{1}{2}$in (9–12mm) spindle gouge

Timber

Straight, well-grained timber is best. Allow an extra $\frac{1}{2}$in (12mm) over the stated mill mechanism length and $\frac{1}{8}$in (3mm) or more on your desired finished diameter size – for example, a mill 8in (203mm) high requires a piece $8\frac{1}{2}$ x $2\frac{3}{8}$ x $2\frac{3}{8}$in (215 x 60 x 60mm). Allow proportional increments for other sizes.

First making stages

Mount the square between centres and turn a true cylinder with a $\frac{3}{4}$in (18mm) roughing gouge or your preferred tool. Use a skew chisel to make each end square.

Now comes your first design decision about the proportion of body to knob – a body length of 6in (152mm) usually gives a good proportion. The prospective base will be made between centres, and the knob on a spigot jaw chuck.

Cut a spigot, 1in (25mm) in diameter and $\frac{1}{8}$in (3mm) long, with a parting tool or skew chisel at the tailstock end. Measure 6in (152mm) from the headstock end and mark with a pencil, then part in, to a depth of about 1in (25mm), with a $\frac{1}{8}$in (3mm) parting tool. Remove the piece from the lathe and cut the top from the base.

Drilling

A pillar drill press is the best tool for the next stage, but you can drill in the lathe if you do not have one. Saw-tooth and Forstner bits make the cleanest cuts and most accurate holes and should be used. Bit sizes of $1\frac{1}{2}$in

(38mm), 1in (25mm) and $\frac{3}{4}$in (18mm) give the best results for the mechanism being used.

Using the drill press, fit the $1\frac{1}{2}$in (38mm) drill in the chuck and set the depth stop to allow a $\frac{1}{4}$in (6mm) deep hole to be cut in the base. Remove this drill, and fit the 1in (25mm) bit in the chuck, setting the drill to cut a hole $\frac{1}{2}$in (12mm) deep in the base recess. Turn your cylinder upside-down and drill centrally down until you are within $\frac{3}{8}$in (9mm) of connecting the two holes through. Remove this drill and fit the $\frac{3}{4}$in (18mm) bit in the chuck and connect the holes. This creates a step on which the stator will rest while allowing the peppercorns to pass through to be ground.

Note: wear a leather-faced glove when you grip the cylinder to protect your palm from burning if the drill grabs.

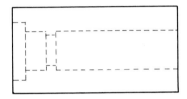

Fig 53 Sequence of holes drilled in the mill base

Turning the body

Select a speed of 1200–1500rpm. Mount the base cylinder between centres. Insert a tapered wooden friction plug in the base to be driven by a four-prong centre in the headstock spindle, while a cone revolving centre in the tailstock should locate in the entrance hole at the top. True any slight inaccuracy at either end with a skew chisel, set a pair of calipers to $2\frac{1}{4}$in (57mm) and skew-chisel the cylinder true.

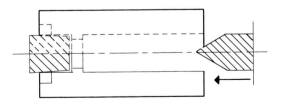

Fig 54 Body mounted between centres, showing the plug and revolving centre

83

Now you are ready to design the base. To create good proportion, it is best if the first elements of the design are positioned no nearer the base than the height of the knob. The knob for this mill is about 1¾in (45mm) long, so the first shaping of the base should not begin below this depth. Mark this first feature of the design with a pencil. The next datum point is possibly the most important because this is where most surface changes begin. A reduction of size by ¼in (6mm) at this point will start to improve the balance, as will a further reduction by another ¼in (6mm) near the top. Check these diameters with calipers. You should now have a three-step cylinder, and shaping can be carried out between these points. The bead is formed with a ⅜in (9mm) beading/parting tool and the main body with the appropriately sized spindle gouges and chisels.

Shaping the base of the pepper mill with a ⅜in (9mm) beading/parting tool

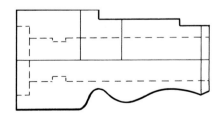

Fig 55 (Top) Body reduced in stages with feature lines marked
(Bottom) Final shape

Sanding and finishing

Hand-sand with the lathe set to the same speed used to turned the mill, using 150, 180 and 240 grit, aluminium oxide, flexible wet and dry abrasive paper. Oil and polish as required, sanding in with worn 320 grit abrasive, before the final finishing and polishing.

Turning the knob

Mount the 1in (25mm) spigot in the appropriate chuck and turn another spigot, exactly the same, on the other end. Check that this spigot will enter the top of the mill base and use a pencil to mark the base's top diameter on the end of this knob, which is a datum point for shaping. Drill a ⁵⁄₁₆in (8mm) hole, about 1in (25mm) deep, in the centre of the knob. Remove the piece from the chuck and turn it round to grip the other spigot. Connect the hole with the ⁵⁄₁₆in (8mm) drill. Reduce the size of the knob so that it is some ⅛in (3mm) smaller than the base's widest diameter. Now fit the stator in the base, pushing the stem mechanism through. Measure the protruding stem at the top of the base to determine the height of the knob. If you have got things right this should be about 1¾in (45mm). Now you can shape a soft, round knob with a spindle gouge and chisel. The incised groove lines are done with the point of a skew chisel.

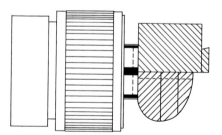

Fig 56 Knob remounted and turned to conclusion

Sanding and finishing

Repeat the processes used for the base.

Assembly

Use small brass screws or brass pins to hold the shaft drive plate and mechanism base bar in place.

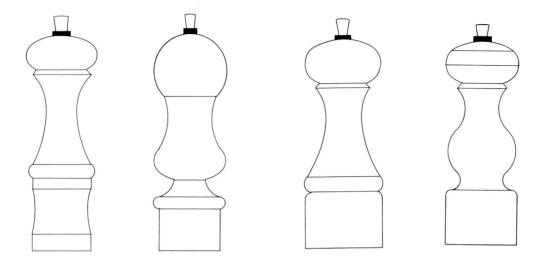

Fig 57a & b Poor designs, with bases too small in diameter, and displaying other features out of proportion

Fig 58a & b Designs with balanced proportions

The pepper mill can be made in varying shapes and sizes following the same basic method

SALAD BOWL

Salad bowl blank mounted on a faceplate; salad bowl with the outside roughly turned

Bowls of all kinds are, perhaps, the most commonly produced items by headstock turners, but they are often unsuccessful in terms of design. Salad bowls seem to be especially unsuccessful. Many bowls lack any shape or sense of balanced form: they are clumpy and clumsy, remaining nothing more than a block of wood with a depression in it. Some look so solid and cumbersome that they give the impression that it would be impossible to lift them from a table. Their bases and walls are often very thick, which means that they do not hold very much, and they are far too heavy for practical use. There are a few obvious do's and don'ts. Anything less than 4in (100mm) high can hardly be called a salad bowl, unless it is a small, individual one intended for a side salad. Base size is important, from the point of view of both design and stability: anything less than one-third of the bowl's greatest diameter will result in poor stability, but anything more than two-thirds will make it difficult to design a shape that has life. Another major don't is never to have the belly of the bowl equidistant between the base and the top, which will produce a dull, lifeless shape. The movement of any curve towards the base or the top will start to give the bowl form.

From a professional producer's point of view, fairly open rather than in-curved or straight-sided forms are easier and quicker to make. This shape also offers more possibilities for producing pleasing designs, and there is also the advantage that such a shape is inherently strong. A cross-grained, curved bowl with a constant wall thickness of ½in (12mm) will be far stronger than a straight-sided bowl of equivalent size. Because the grain runs horizontal to the base, it will sometimes lengthen through the curve to as much as ¾in (18mm), whereas there will be no increase in strength of a straight-sided one. Any knock on the end grain makes it more susceptible to damage and splitting. It is worth remembering that curved shapes are always stronger than straight ones.

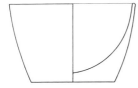

Fig 59 Drastic example of poor form, unfortunately not uncommon

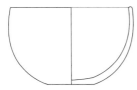

Fig 60 Bowl of improved proportions; the base is almost half of the maximum diameter

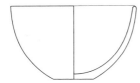

Fig 61 Good form, with base one-third of the maximum diameter

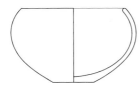

Fig 62 Again a good form, incurved with a base size of one-third of the diameter

```
SUGGESTED LATHE TOOLS

Faceplate or faceplate ring
Expansion-contraction jaw chuck
½in (12mm) deep fluted bowl gouge
⅛in (3mm) parting tool
1¼in (31mm) square-ended scraper
½in (12mm) Key spindle gouge (modified)
½in (12mm) Key skew chisel (modified)
1½in (38mm) Key French curve scraper
Note: all 'Key-type' tools can be ground to similar
shapes from standard tools
'Bowl saving' Stewart slicer or Kel McNaughton system
```

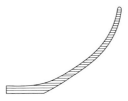

Fig 63 Constant wall thickness, showing how the strength is improved through a curved arc

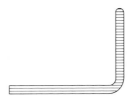

Fig 64 Constant wall thickness but with no improvement in strength

Timber selection and preparation

It is almost impossible to buy from any source dry timber in the thickness required for a salad bowl – that is, 4in (100mm) upwards. I prefer to buy large, complete logs in the round (mostly ash) and have these converted into planks 4in (100mm) and 6in (150mm) thick. Most of you are far more likely to buy pre-cut discs that have been hot-waxed sealed however. Such wood is normally labelled 'part dry', although to me this means quite wet. (The terms 'part dry' or 'unseasoned' wood should be interpreted as having a 30–80 per cent moisture content. Kiln-dried or seasoned wood should be regarded as having a 10–20 per cent moisture content.)

For the purposes of describing the making of this salad bowl, it is assumed that you are using unseasoned wood, bought as a pre-cut disc. Remember that any size of disc bought this way will produce a finished bowl with a diameter ¾–1in (18–25mm) smaller than the original disc. There are a number of variables here, ranging from how much wood you turn away, to the moisture content of the wood and the point the disc was cut from the log.

Outside roughing

Mount a faceplate or faceplate ring on what is to be the top of your bowl, and mount the disc on the lathe. Proceed to shape the bowl at a safe speed, using a ½in (12mm) bowl gouge. Your cuts can be quite aggressive, because the wood is moist and cuts easily, offering little resistance. Cut from the base towards the top of your bowl, holding the gouge flute towards you, at an angle of 45 degrees out of the vertical, with the bevel rubbing to support the cut.

Once you have a shape you are happy with, mark a diameter on the base with dividers or a pencil. This should be compatible with the size of your bowl and with one of

the expanding chuck jaw sets you need for this project. Take a parting tool and cut in on your marked line to a depth of about ¼in (6mm). Create the core recess with the gouge and true this flat with a scraper. You need to cut a dovetail angle on the opening so that the jaws will locate in it, and this is best done with the point of a ½in (12mm) Key skew chisel, held flat on the rest and used like a scraper. Remove the piece from the lathe.

Shaping the inside

Mount your bowl on the expanding jaw chuck and make it secure. If you have a large bowl blank it is worth saving a core from its centre as shown in the photograph below. This was done with the Stewart slicer. You open up a slot with the tool, cutting in at an angle to produce a cone. When you feel that this is weak enough, remove the bowl from the chuck. Place the bowl in a bed of shavings and use a heavy hammer to give a sharp tap near the edge of the inner core, which should break out. This leaves you with another, smaller bowl blank that would otherwise have been shavings.

Remount the bowl on the chuck and hollow it out with a ½in (12mm) bowl gouge, cutting from the top towards the base. The flute of the gouge should be facing away from you, at an angle of 45 degrees out of the vertical, and

The centre of the bowl can be saved if it is large enough

its bevel should support the cut. Aim to create a consistent wall thickness: bowls from 10 x 4in (255 x 100mm) up to 19 x 6in (482 x 150mm) are roughed out, leaving a wall thickness of $1-1\frac{1}{2}$in (25–38mm). These dimensions will allow you to make finished bowls after distortion in drying has taken place normally that have a wall thickness of $\frac{3}{8}-\frac{1}{2}$in (9–12mm) and $\frac{5}{8}-\frac{3}{4}$in (15–18mm), respectively. Remove the bowl from the lathe.

Drying

The method described here is the way I like to work. First, weigh the roughed-out bowl and use a pencil to note the weight and date on the side. Place it to dry near the floor in a cool area that is out of direct sunlight and draughts – a corner of your workshop should be fine. If the bowl is exposed to sunlight or draughts, end cracks, splits and so on can occur, and if you have any doubts, it is better to apply PVA or wax to the end grain to stop the wood drying out too fast. Weigh the bowl every week or so, and make a note of the new weight and the date. Most moisture evaporates in the first two weeks, and as the bowl steadily dries, you can move it higher and into a warmer environment. The length of time needed for the piece to dry out will depend on a variety of factors, including the drying area, the time of year, the type of timber and how

wet it was to begin with. Six weeks would be quick; eight to ten weeks is usual; and almost anything left for three months will be dry. Remember, though, that the moisture content of anything can only ever go down to the humidity of the atmosphere in which it is stored.

If you use a dehumidifying chamber for drying, you should normally exect the cycle to take thirty to forty-five days, depending on the timbers being dried.

Final outside shaping

Your dry bowl should now be ready for final turning. If the distortion has been very great, you may need to re-cut the recess to make it true. There are many ways of doing this, and you can use any method you like. I usually grip the rim of the bowl in a set of home-made wooden jaws. These mount on to jaw plates that fit the Axminster four-jaw chuck and are contracted down to grip the rim of the bowl. This is the chuck I use for the majority of my reverse-chucking. Re-cut the recess as required.

Remove the bowl from the lathe. Change over to your expanding jaw chuck and secure your bowl on this. You will now need to re-cut the outside bowl shape true after the distortion caused during the drying process. Use a $\frac{1}{2}$in (12mm) bowl gouge, with its wings ground back, to do this,

Final outside shaping with a $\frac{1}{2}$in (12mm) Key spindle gouge

with the gouge flute angled towards you at 45 degrees out of the vertical, with the bevel rubbing cut from the base to the top. To cut, hold the gouge handle in the left hand. Push with this hand and pull the blade with the right hand.

Once it is true, the refined finishing cuts are made with a Key ½in (12mm) modified spindle gouge. I use this tool to finish the outside of 95 per cent of all the bowls I make. The handle is held in the right hand and angled downwards. The heel near the tip of the gouge is brought into contact near the base of the bowl. No more than the first ¼–⅜in (6–9mm) of this tip side heel should ever be in contact with the bowl as the cutting proceeds. Pull the gouge from the base to the top of the bowl with a slicing action – you should aim to produce a fine ribbon shaving, with the bevel supporting the cutting tip throughout. This type of cut is the nearest equivalent in headstock work to a chisel cut in spindle work. With practice, you should achieve a fine, clean surface, free of grain pull or roughness, that is ready for sanding.

The top and inside

The top should be turned true with the bowl gouge. The hollowing inside the bowl is completed with the ½in (12mm) bowl gouge with the wings ground back. The method is the same as in the roughing-out process but is far less aggressive. Try to cut with continuous, fluid movements from the top to the base of the bowl. Position your feet and distribute your body weight to give good balance. Try not to move your feet during the cutting action because it will lead to broken, stepped and rippled tool work.

Despite your best efforts, it will be inevitable that there are some odd ripples and undulations in the salad bowl that must be removed with a fine scraper. Make light passing cuts with a Key French curve scraper. Cup the outside of the bowl with your left hand to absorb any vibration or flex, then set the rest high enough to allow the scraper to cut at centre height when it is tilted down 10–15 degrees out of the horizontal during cutting. Push the scraper from the top of the bowl towards the base, which will eliminate almost all outward side pressure. This is to be avoided at all costs because it can lead to chatter and grain tear, and in extreme cases it can grab and shatter the bowl. Remember to use light, very fine pushing cuts.

Light passing cuts removing ripples with a Key French curve scraper

Sanding and oiling

You are now ready to sand to finish. I power-sand inside and outside using 3in (75mm) Velcro-backed pads and discs. If you have used a coarse-grained wood, start sanding with 80 grit abrasive, before working through the 120, 180 and 240 grit grades. Give the bowl a liberal coat of oil, and hand-sand with worn 240 grit flexible cloth-backed aluminium abrasive. Apply another liberal coat of oil and burnish it in with fine finish cut shavings. Remove the bowl from the lathe ready to finish the base.

Finishing the base

Reverse-chuck and grip your bowl. Make the bottom slightly concave and create a nice, soft, flowing curve instead of the hard edge that exists where the dovetail chuck gripped the bowl. Tool this area with a gouge and scraper, before sanding and oiling.

The Key reverse-chucking bowl device

Completed salad bowls made in ash in a range of sizes

INDIVIDUAL ITEMS

Have clear aims when you start to make 'one-off' pieces. Consider what makes an individual piece. I like purity of line, not gimmicks and prefer to concentrate on objects that are made to give visual pleasure, but most woodturners compromise, producing items that are recognizable as useful – bowls, platters and boxes – and this seems to be the only way to survive financially. Some people must assure themselves before they buy an object that it could be put to use if necessary, although it is designed to give visual pleasure. All too often woodturners forget the importance of shape and form and are seduced by the beauty of the material, but highly figured woods must be made into forms that reflect their inherent beauty. When someone admires the form or shape before commenting on the wood, you have succeeded.

Burr oak vessel

BOXES

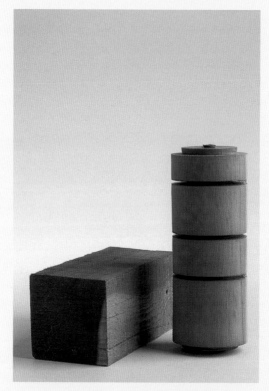

Spigot lid box blank ready for turning; the blank rough turned into
a cylinder with main divisions incised

My thoughts about making beautiful objects may seem a
little at odds with the next projects. Boxes are normally
regarded as functional items, and there is no doubt that
the pieces described here will hold jewellery, pills and so
on. However, my prime aim is to produce aesthetically
pleasing items, and I would hope that the best of these
could be viewed as miniature works of art.

What makes a good box? I avoid grain mismatch;
wherever possible, I design each piece so that the inside
form follows the contours of the outside; and I insist that
the craftsmanship and finish are of the highest standard
both inside and out. The fit of the lid is important: when a
box is turned upside-down, the lid should not fall off, but it

should not be so tight that force is required to remove it.
The best results are achieved by using end-grained
material, and you will find that pieces that are more than
4in (100mm) in diameter will make it difficult to obtain a
good snug lid fit, because atmospheric changes affect
stability. Most of the boxes I make are 2–3in (50–75mm)
in diameter, and I prefer dense, close-grained hardwoods
that are dry – that is, they have less than 10 per cent
moisture content.

The proportions vary, but I have found that the most
successful boxes are in the ratio of two-fifths lid to three-
fifths base. I would say that 75 per cent of my designs
have these proportions.

SPIGOT LID BOX

SUGGESTED LATHE TOOLS

Four-prong drive centre

Revolving ring centre

Four-jaw chuck or contracting dovetail chuck

1in (25mm) O'Donnell jaws

$\frac{3}{4}$in (18mm) roughing gouge

$\frac{1}{16}$–$\frac{1}{8}$in (2–3mm) parting tool

$\frac{3}{8}$in (9mm) spindle gouge

$\frac{3}{8}$in (9mm) beading/parting tool

$\frac{3}{8}$in (9mm) Key modified spindle gouge

$\frac{1}{2}$in (12mm) Key skew chisel

$\frac{3}{4}$in (18mm) Key end- and side-cutting scraper

Timber selection and preparation

Straight-grained, dense, dry hard wood is required for this box, which has straight, rounded corners. I usually make two boxes from one piece $5\frac{1}{2}$ x 2 x 2in (140 x 50 x 50mm) in size, and the instructions below are based on this premise. Although these instructions are for making a straight, rounded corner, spigot-lid box, the procedures are the same for all boxes with this type of lid – the major difference is that more tooling and shaping are necessary in most of them.

Saw a cross, about $\frac{1}{8}$in (3mm) deep, in the end of your square into which your four-prong drive centre will locate. Do not hammer a drive centre into the end because dense wood may split. Mount the square between centres: a four-prong in the headstock locates in your saw cuts, and a revolving ring centre in the tailstock. Rough the square into a cylinder with a $\frac{3}{4}$in (18mm) roughing gouge, with the speed set to 1300–1500rpm. Use a parting tool or spindle gouge or the point of a skew chisel to true each end square and slightly concave. This is all you need to do at this stage if you use my method of holding, which is by means of the Axminster four-jaw self-centring chuck with engineer's jaws fitted. Any three- or four-jaw engineer's chuck will do. If you do not have one of these, you will need to cut a dovetail spigot at each end. The spigot

should be about $\frac{1}{8}$in (3mm) long and 1–$1\frac{1}{2}$in (25–38mm) in diameter to locate in a compatible contracting jaw chuck. Remove your cylinder and drive centres from the lathe.

Chucking and proportions

Mount the chuck in the lathe and close down the chuck jaws on to the cylinder. Tool the drive centre marks from the end. If the cylinder is running slightly out of true, correct this inaccuracy now.

The first decisions about proportion must now be made. The cylinder is now nearer $1\frac{7}{8}$in (48mm) in diameter, and a finished height of about 2in (50mm) will look well. Bearing in mind the ideal ratio of two-fifths to three-fifths, it is time to mark out the cylinder with a pencil line ready for parting in cuts. Mark $\frac{3}{4}$in (18mm) down from the top, which makes the visual size of the base about $1\frac{1}{4}$in (31mm). Now you must remember to add the width of the parting tool and the length of the spigot to this dimension. If this is $\frac{3}{8}$in (9mm), this will enable you to use a $\frac{1}{16}$–$\frac{1}{8}$in (2–3mm) parting tool to part the lid off and still leave enough timber for a $\frac{1}{4}$–$\frac{5}{16}$in (6–7mm) spigot. With these dimensions taken into consideration, you can part the lid off. Remove the remaining cylinder from the chuck.

Lid hollowing

Invert the lid into the chuck ready for hollowing. True the parting cut end with a gouge or skew chisel, then set a depth gauge to leave $\frac{1}{8}$in (3mm) thickness in the lid's top. Now start to hollow the lid with the Key $\frac{3}{8}$in (9mm) modified spindle gouge, using the same procedure as for the salt bowl (see pages 73-4). Position the tool rest across the face of the lid, just below centre height, and present the gouge to the centre of the lid with its open face towards you, horizontal and parallel to the bed. Tilt the face of the gouge away from you so that it is 10–15 degrees out of the vertical. Now push in towards the headstock. You will find that the gouge acts like a drill. Make sure you do not go too deep; check with your depth gauge. Now tilt the gouge 45 degrees out of the vertical and, making a series of pivoting and scooping cuts, open and deepen the recess in the lid. As you work, the short bevel rubs and supports the cutting edge. Some 95 to 98 per cent of the lid's interior can be removed in this way.

True any ripples caused by the gouge with a ¾in (18mm) Key end- and side-cutting scraper, which has a small radius on the left-hand corner. Take light cuts from the centre outwards, then draw the tool towards you, up the side wall, aiming for a thickness of ⅛in (3mm). It is important that the sides are square. If you are in any doubt, slightly undercut. Never taper inwards, which will make it impossible for the lid to fit snugly on the base.

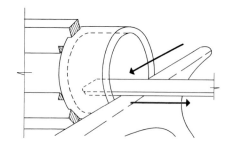

Fig 65 Scraping from the centre outwards and pulling up the side wall

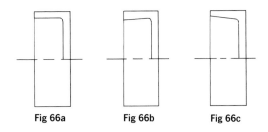

| Fig 66a | Fig 66b | Fig 66c |

Fig 66a Correct lid form
Fig 66b Works but incorrect
Fig 66c Unacceptable

Lid sanding and finishing

Sand the lid with narrow strips of 150, 180, 240, 320 and 400 grit soft-flex aluminium oxide abrasive. I dip the abrasive in wax to minimize friction heat and dust. Be careful not to round the opening of the lid. Finally, finish with 0000 steel wool or ultra-fine Scotch-Brite pads dipped in wax and buff to a satin lustre with a polishing cloth.

All these procedures take place with the lathe rotating at 1300–1500rpm. Remove the lid from the chuck.

Lid fitting

Replace the cylinder into the chuck and tool the parted end clean. Set a vernier to the inside lid measurement. This will give you a guide, but the tight, snug fit you want is almost unmeasurable. Use a ⅜in (9mm) beading/parting tool to start to cut the spigot for the lid to fit on. Aim to fit the lid on a 1⁄16–⅛in (2–3mm) long spigot at first, just in case you cut too small. Once the fit is right, lengthen it to 3⁄16–¼in (5–6mm). Your lid should be a nice friction fit.

Outside shaping

With the lid in place, part in to a depth of ¼–⅜in (6–9mm) on the headstock side of your base length pencil line. True the outside of the box clean with a chisel or the ⅜in (9mm) Key modified spindle gouge (this is my preferred tool on exotic and difficult woods). True the top of the box with a ⅜in (9mm) spindle gouge, removing any ripples with the ½in (12mm) Key skew, used flat on the rest like a scraper. Round the corners at the top and base with a ⅜in (9mm) spindle gouge, and, finally, refine them with the ⅜in (9mm) beading/parting tool.

Remove the lid and cut a little gap line, about 1⁄16in (2mm) deep and wide, with the ⅜in (9mm) beading/parting tool. This line will take the eye through any mismatch of grain caused by the removal of the ⅜in (9mm) that happens with the parting off and spigot length. It also is instantly apparent which is the top and which is the base.

Base hollowing

Now hollow out the base in exactly the same way as you did the lid – use the same methods and the same tools. The base and walls should be 3⁄16in (5mm) thick, which will give you a 1⁄16in (2mm) spigot thickness. Replace the lid.

Sanding and finishing

Sand the exterior first. Remove the lid and sand the interior. Apply wax on 0000 steel wool or an ultra-fine Scotch-Brite pad, then buff to a satin lustre with a soft polishing cloth. Do not sand the spigot or this will give

Truing up gouge ripples with a
Key end side-cutting scraper

you a loose lid, although you may wish to apply wax and polish.

Parting off

Almost part off the box from the remaining cylinder, but stop ⅛–³⁄₁₆in (3–5mm) from doing so or there is a risk of torquing and pulling a hole through the base. Use a saw to cut it from the cylinder.

Finishing the base

Remove the remaining cylinder from the chuck and replace it with a block of waste material. Cut a spigot over which the base will go, making sure that this is a good friction fit. Carefully tool the base with a spindle gouge and ½in (12mm) Key skew chisel as described above for finishing the lid. Sand and polish as for the remainder of the box.

Making the next box

Remove the waste block, replace the cylinder, tool the end clean and part off a lid. Remove the base element from the chuck and invert it. Cut a small spigot to fit the 1in (25mm) O'Donnell spigot jaws or your chosen chuck. There are two reasons for doing this: saving timber and safety. If the tooling of the outside of this second box were carried out in a normal engineer's chuck, your knuckles and fingers would be very close to the jaws. Remove the base and insert the lid and proceed through all the stages described for the first box.

The lid is held in the engineer's jaws to hollow out the inside as in the first box, then tooled and sanded. Remove the lid at this stage and also the engineer's jaws, replacing them with a set of O'Donnell jaws which allow you to work safely as they form a smooth continuous cone.

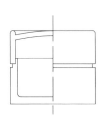

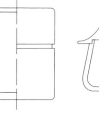

Fig 67 Beaded, squat box   **Fig 68** Hard, squat box   **Fig 69** Sun hat box   **Fig 70** Capsule box   **Fig 71** Bowler hat box

Completed box made in cocobolo

Two boxes based on the same design principles and made
in kingwood (left) and Brazilian tulipwood (right).

FINIAL LID BOX

When it comes to making this kind of box, there are a number of differences, in both the design proportion and the making procedures, compared with boxes with spigot lids.

The proportions are different because the visual lid length is one-third long to the two-thirds of the base. The making is different because you make just one box from your cylinder, and this is not removed until the box is almost complete (if you have two chucks, that is).

SUGGESTED LATHE TOOLS

Four-prong drive centre
Revolving ring centre
Contracting spigot jaw chuck
Axminster four-jaw chuck with 1in (25mm)
  O'Donnell jaws
$\frac{3}{4}$in (18mm) roughing gouge
$\frac{3}{8}$in (9mm) spindle gouge
$\frac{3}{8}$in (9mm) beading/parting tool
$\frac{3}{8}$in (9mm) Key spindle gouge (modified)
$\frac{1}{16}$in (2mm) Key parting tool
$\frac{1}{2}$in (12mm) Key skew chisel
$\frac{3}{4}$in (18mm) Key round-side cutting scraper
$\frac{3}{4}$in (18mm) Key round cutaway scraper

Timber selection and preparation

Timber is much the same as for the spigot boxes: you should use straight-grained, dry, dense hardwood. One box is made from a piece of wood $4\frac{1}{2}$–$4\frac{3}{4}$ x $2\frac{1}{4}$ x $2\frac{1}{4}$in (115–120 x 58 x 58mm), and this is an ideal size.

Use a saw to cut a cross in one end in which a small four-prong drive centre can locate. Mount the block between centres – four-prong in the headstock and revolving ring in the tailstock – and set the speed at 1300–1500rpm to rough the block to a cylinder with a $\frac{3}{4}$in (18mm) roughing gouge. True each end square with a parting tool, spindle gouge or the point of a skew chisel. At the headstock end cut a spigot that is no more than $\frac{1}{8}$in (3mm) long and 1in (25mm) in diameter. Cut a slight

Finial box blank; final box with shaping almost complete

undercut dovetail on this that is compatible with the contraction jaws on your chuck. (I use an Axminster self-centring four-jaw with 1in (25mm) O'Donnell spigot jaws fitted.) The cylinder is held in this way to make the complete box. Remove the cylinder and drive centres from the lathe.

Chucking and proportions

Mount your chuck with spigot jaws and close these down on the spigot. If the cylinder is running slightly out of true, correct it at this point. Now is the time to mark out the proportions. Visually, the lid will be one-third of the length, and the base will be two-thirds, but you must remember to add the fit-in plug length, which will work out at about $\frac{1}{4}$in (6mm). The visual length of the finial will be about $1\frac{1}{4}$in (31mm), so you need to mark a pencil line $1\frac{1}{2}$–$1\frac{9}{16}$in (38–40mm) in from the unsupported end. Part in at the headstock side of your pencil line to a depth of about $\frac{5}{8}$in (15mm) with a $\frac{1}{16}$–$\frac{1}{8}$in (2–3mm) narrow parting tool.

Finial shaping

Set a pair of calipers to 1¼in (31mm) and reduce the knob to this size with a ⅜in (9mm) spindle gouge. Mark a pencil line ¼in (6mm) up from the parting cut. Now shape 95 per cent of the finial form with the spindle gouge and refine with the ⅜in (9mm) beading/parting tool. The beading/parting tool, used in the manner of a chisel, should be used to tool the ¼in (6mm) plug area parallel. This area only is polished at this stage, because this is the only opportunity you have to do so. Carefully part the knob off.

Shaping with a ⅜in (9mm) spindle gouge

Underside of the lid

For several years I did no more than disc-sand and polish the underside of the lid. For the last ten years, however, I have reverse-chucked lids and tooled the underside. Although this adds a little to the making time, it does produce a superior article. I use two methods to do this, both of which involve inverting the knob. The better method uses a home-made wooden, hollow, mandrel chuck; the quicker method uses a contracting metal jaw chuck. The metal jaws can mark the plug, so protect it with some paper towel or rag. Tool the underside of the lid with the ⅜in (9mm) spindle gouge to make it slightly concave and use the ½in (12mm) Key skew like a scraper to remove ripples. Sand and polish to finish before removing from the chuck.

Fitting the lid

Clean the cut made by the parting tool on the top of the base to make it true, before marking the diameter of the lid plug. Start to remove some of the base interior with the ⅜in (9mm) Key modified spindle gouge, following the instructions for hollowing the box with the spigot lid (see pages 95–7). You need to cut a shoulder about ¼in (6mm) deep on which the lid can bottom out. I use the ⅜in (9mm) beading/parting tool for this. Your aim is for a precise friction fit, so that when the lid is removed there is a suction 'pop' noise. The lid should be slightly proud of the body at this stage.

Shaping the body and lid together

The friction fit of the lid enables you to shape and blend the body and lid together, and I find that a ⅜in (9mm) spindle gouge are ideal for this. Truing and refining the shape and surface are carried out with the ⅜in (9mm) beading/parting tool, which should be used like a chisel. You should be aiming to create three-quarters of the finished profile at this stage, but the area near the base should be left thicker for the moment to provide strength and support when the inside is hollowed out.

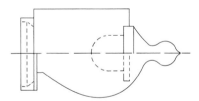

Fig 72 Top: body with lid fitted on shoulder; bottom: lid/knob blended into a three-quarter-formed body

Hollowing the base

Remove the lid and use the gouge to hollow the base as previously described. Set your depth gauge so that it is about ⁵⁄₁₆in (7mm) short of the chuck, which allows for a ⅛in (3mm) parting tool to be used and leave ³⁄₁₆in (5mm) in the base. Be careful with your hollowing: the careless use of tools can result in damage to the shoulder and entrance hole. The gouge can be used to remove 95 per cent of the interior, and any ripples caused by the gouge can be removed with the Key round-side cutting scraper and the Key round cutaway scraper. The round cutaway tool enables you to get under the shoulder and minimizes the chance of fouling the tool on the far side of the opening. The round-side cutting tool is fed to the bottom of the box. With the rest set at the right height, gently draw it towards you and manipulate it carefully to remove the ripples on the way. The interior is now completely tooled.

Final shaping of the body

Part in a short way above the chuck jaws with a $\frac{1}{16}$–$\frac{1}{8}$in (2–3mm) parting tool. Replace the lid and start to shape the rest of the outside of the body, using the $\frac{3}{8}$in (9mm) spindle gouge and the $\frac{3}{8}$in (9mm) beading/parting tools.

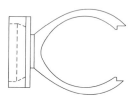

Fig 73 The inside completed using a gouge and Key Scraper

You may feel the lid has no part to play in this sequence, but it is important that it is in place, because it allows you to see the complete profile, which makes it easier to create a well-balanced form.

Sanding and polishing

Sand outside and inside the box with 150, 180, 240, 320 and 400 grit, soft-flex, aluminium oxide papers dipped in

Completing the body shape with a $\frac{3}{8}$in beading tool

wax to minimize friction heat and dust. The final smoothing is done with 0000 steel wool or ultra-fine Scotch-Brite pads. Finish by waxing and buffing with a soft polishing cloth.

A lathe speed of 1300–1500rpm is suggested throughout the making of this box.

Finishing the bottom

Part almost through and saw off. Secure a waste block in a chuck and cut a spigot onto which the lid recess in the base will friction fit. Tool the bottom with a spindle gouge and Key skew chisel as previously explained. Sand and polish and your box is complete.

Note: Reverse chucking of all boxes is best carried out on timber that is softer and coarser grained than the box being finished off. This ensures a better grip and reduces the risk of splitting a box.

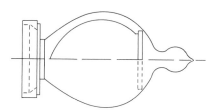

Fig 74 Box almost complete. It just needs parting off and the base finished

Completed finial box made in yew

A range of finial lid boxes made in, from left to right, yew, olivewood, kingwood and olivewood again

PLATTERS

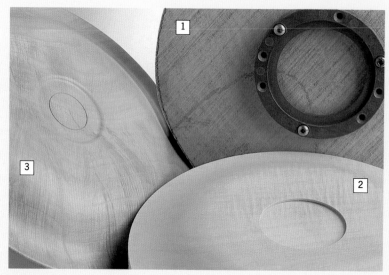

The platter prepared for turning: mounted on a faceplate ring (1), prepared for mounting on an expanding dovetail chuck (2), and base tooled to conclusion (3)

Platters are made from slim discs of wood, which means there are fewer design options when it comes to shape. The rim and flange areas provide opportunity for expression, however, and the limitations on the shape enable the turner to make an object that can be beautiful and functional without having to compromise.

When you buy boards or planks, areas of ripple, burr, crotch, quilt or stain are often found in boards that are predominantly plain. This is where the maker who produces both functional and one-off pieces can sometimes have the best of both worlds, and when it happens to me, I mark out the areas of real beauty, aiming for the largest possible piece. I would rather obtain one large item that reveals the true splendour of the timber than dilute it by trying to obtain two or more smaller ones, even though it is often easier to sell the smaller pieces than the larger ones.

Making a platter is a fairly straightforward exercise for a competent headstock turner, but it is amazing how few really good ones you see. The most common faults found in platters are:

- Surfaces are often rippled and uneven.
- Blended curves often lack transitional fluidity, being abrupt or hooked.
- The bases of the exterior and interior are often convex instead of slightly concave.

- Bases are often too thick while flanges are frequently too thin.
- Detail work is often applied to unsuitable coarse-grained materials, resulting in torn grain, and even when suitable materials are selected, the detailing often lacks refinement – for example, little flats on beads instead of nicely rounded ones.
- When a footring is applied (and my own opinion is that they should be reserved for dishes and bowls) it should be between two-fifths and one-third of the overall diameter.

The following guidelines should always be observed if you want to produce a successful platter:

- Always turn the exterior first.
- The base should be slightly concave, allowing for the largest diameter to rest on any surface. This will stop spinning and rocking.
- If a flange is part of your design, it should not be thinner than $\frac{5}{32}$in (4mm), or it will look weak. The top surface of the flange should tilt in slightly towards the middle to give the platter life and poise.
- The interior surface should not be rippled or uneven, and it should be flat or slightly concave, not convex.
- All transitional curves should be smoothly blended.
- Detail work should be crisp and refined and in proportion with the overall design.
- Flamboyant materials do not require elaborate design: let the wood speak, and keep the form and any surface decoration simple.

SUGGESTED LATHE TOOLS

Faceplate or faceplate ring or screw chuck
Expanding dovetail jaw chuck
$\frac{1}{2}$in (12mm) bowl gouge
1–1$\frac{1}{4}$in (25–31mm) square-ended scraper
1–1$\frac{1}{4}$in (25–31mm) curved-ended scraper
$\frac{1}{8}$in (3mm) parting tool
$\frac{1}{2}$in (12mm) Key skew chisel
1$\frac{1}{2}$in (38mm) Key/Nish shear scraper

Chucking

Mount your disc on a faceplate, faceplate ring or screw chuck.

Outside turning

A sycamore disc, 12 x 1$\frac{1}{4}$in (305 x 31mm), was used to make the platter illustrated here. A speed of 800–1000rpm is ideal. True the outside diameter with a $\frac{1}{2}$in (12mm) bowl gouge, with its flute held at an angle of 45 degrees out of the vertical and the bevel rubbing.

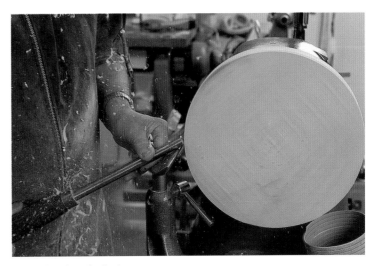

Shaping the edge with a bowl gouge

Move the tool rest across the base and true this in the same way. I generally cut initially from the middle towards the edge, because this provides a surface on which to rest the bevel. It is also a much safer way of working than from the edge towards the middle, because any distortion and warping of the material make it difficult to judge the depth of cut. Once all the distortion high spots have been removed, you can cut either way. Use the gouge to make the base true, then mark a line with dividers ready to cut a recess to accept an expanding jaw chuck – one with a 2$\frac{3}{4}$in (70mm) diameter is ideal. Cut this to a depth of $\frac{3}{16}$in (5mm) with a $\frac{1}{8}$in (3mm) parting tool. The core recess is removed with the gouge and lightly tooled flat with a square-ended scraper, and the dovetail undercut is done with the point of the $\frac{1}{2}$in (12mm) Key skew chisel, used flat on the rest.

The shaping of the base profile into a subtle ogee curve is done with the ½in (12mm) bowl gouge used as previously described. This creates 95 to 98 per cent of the profile.Final refinements to the surface are best done with a 1½in (38mm) Key/Nish shear scraper, held so that it is tilted out of the vertical, at an angle of 30–45 degrees. Before I had a shear scraper I would have used a square-ended scraper and a curve-ended one, both used flat on the rest and cutting at centre height, and then tilted them down 10–15 degrees out of the vertical. But the shear scraper cut gives a cleaner finish.

Shaping the base with a Key/Nish shear scraper

Sanding

I prefer to power-sand the main shape, using 3in (75mm) Velcro-backed pads and discs and working through 120, 180, 240 and 400 grit. I hand-sand the recess using similar grits of soft-flex, aluminium oxide papers. The final abrasion is done with hand-held, ultra-fine Scotch-Brite pads.

Finishing

A thin coat of pre-cat satin lacquer is applied with a mop brush, and allowed to dry for 15–18 hours.

The platter is returned to the lathe and the sealer is cut back with 400 grit, soft-flex, aluminium oxide paper, dipped in wax. This is followed by an ultra-fine Scotch-Brite pad, which has been dipped in wax to help prevent lacquer melt and drag. This process will prevent lacquer rings and build-up, and you can then buff the platter with a soft cloth to a satin lustre. Remove from the chuck.

Turning the inside

Mount and secure the platter on your expanding jaw chuck and make sure that everything runs true. True the face in exactly the same way as you tooled the base – that is, cut from the centre towards the edge with the gouge until it is true. Mark your flange width with a pencil – 1¼–1½in (31–38mm) is fine – then use the gouge to begin to hollow the platter interior away from this line. Hollow only to a depth of ¼–⅜in (6–9mm) at the moment.

Now come back to the top of the flange and tool this true with the gouge. Finally, make very light cuts with a square-ended scraper or the Key/Nish shear scraper tool. Your fingers should be behind the flange, steadying it, damping down tool noise and absorbing any vibration. Any design detail on the flange should be done now, before you complete the hollowing of the interior.

Shaping the inside of the platter with a 1⁄2in (12mm) square across ground bowl gouge

Continue to deepen the interior with the bowl gouge until you are close to your desired depth. A base thickness of ⁵⁄₁₆–⅜in (8–10mm) is recommended. At this stage, change the way you use the gouge. I use a square-ground gouge with a bevel angle of 55–65 degrees, and this allows me to take finishing cuts with the tool in a more horizontal plane. The flute becomes almost horizontal, too, as the back wing of the tool takes fine planing cuts. This technique needs practice, but once you have mastered it, you will be able to cut much truer, flatter surfaces with a gouge than in any other way. Any necessary surface blending can be done with the appropriate scrapers.

Sanding

The flange should be hand-sanded in the same way as the recess in the base. The interior is power-sanded in the same way as the outside profile. Take care that you do not dwell in the centre with the discs, or you will abrade a depression. The final abrasion is with an ultra-fine Scotch-Brite pad.

Fig 75   Simple flange

Fig 76   Simple flange but with an incision framing the opening

Fig 77   Undercut rim for a dish which creates shadow

Fig 78   Undercut rim for a platter which creates shadow

Fig 79   Reflex curve but opening framed-in tension

Fig 80   Applied single bead

Fig 81   Applied single bead framing the opening

Fig 82   Inset stepped cove

Fig 83   Double inset stepped cove

Fig 84   Series of inset beads

Fig 85   Series of applied beads

Fig 86   Opening framed by a bold inset bead

Fig 87   Opening framed by a stepped inset cove

Finishing

This is exactly the same process as that used for the outside. Once it is completed, remove the platter from the chuck.

Reverse-chucking

This is the final procedure. I use a wooden four-jaw plate chuck for this, closing the jaws down on to the flange. The hard dovetail chuck jaw recess is softened into a fluid curve with a gouge, hand-sanded and polished as previously described. Remove from the chuck and your platter is complete.

Finished platter made in bird's-eye maple wood with shaped bead inside edge profile

Alternative style of platter with wide rim made in rippled/quilted olive ash

BOWLS

Three ways to divide a small log to produce different size bowls and varied effects

Making individual bowls provides the turner with one of the greatest areas of freedom to express preferences in shape and design and it offers opportunities to use timbers of all sorts and sizes. The possibilities are limited only by the maker's imagination.

Throughout this section the photographs and drawings illustrate objects that have a strong aesthetic appeal, but they also reflect a progressive approach, both in terms of difficulty in making and in the creative use of the material. When bowls that are strong in visual appeal are made, the importance of function is often overlooked, especially the base size formula.

One of the first actions in a non-functional bowl is to turn the walls so that they are much thinner than is

Fig 88 Thin-walled bowl with small base

Fig 89 Thin-walled bowl with small foot

practical for use. It is also usual to give such a bowl a small foot or base. The combination of these two factors leads the turner to produce delicate but, ideally, strong aesthetic forms.

Timber choice

The choice of wood and the way it is cut are very important in bowl-making. Woods that have great inherent beauty call for a sensitive response that will reflect, use and complement nature through the forms and shapes that are created.

In my own bowl-making, I cover a wide spectrum, from the small and delicate to the large and rugged. The types of timber I use are equally varied, ranging from pure white holly to jet black ebony. Each kind works differently and each presents its own challenges. The smell, texture and colour contribute to the fascination of working with wood, each element combining with the others to create a unique experience every time.

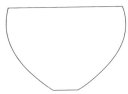

Fig 90 Bowl showing easy flowing curves

Fig 91 Bowl showing too flat a lower section curve in relationship to that in the upper section, resulting in an unbalanced piece

Fig 92 Bowl from large log, through-sawn

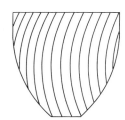

Fig 93 Bowl from large log, quarter-sawn

Growth rings

Delicate small bowls are best made from woods that are slow grown, so that any growth ring pattern will enhance rather than overpower the beauty of the form. Many of the light-coloured woods have very little growth ring figure, so there are no restrictions on size, shape or design.

Fig 94 Small bowl reflecting the growth rings

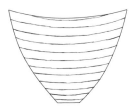

Fig 95 Similar to Fig 94, but with the edge shaped, giving an added aesthetic appeal

Sapwood

Sapwood is usually removed, particularly when the timber is to be used for structural and furniture purposes, because it is normally softer and weaker than heartwood. It is also more susceptible to worm attack and decay. In woodturning, however, this characteristic is not a problem when used to make decorative bowls, for which it can be used to dramatic effect. Many dark woods display a considerable contrast between their heartwood and sapwood, none more so than African blackwood (see the photograph overleaf). It should be noted, too, that the sapwood of many exotic woods is often harder than the heartwood of many temperate hardwoods.

The bowls in this section were made from a small cherry log, and there is little contrast between the sapwood and heartwood in timbers of this type. However, different approaches to cutting and turning make it possible to achieve a variety of different results.

Decorative use of sapwood for a bowl made in African blackwood

those that are dramatic and rugged. The photographs and illustration below reveal some of the ways such wood can be used. Burrs offer spectacular grain formation, and it is all too easy to be seduced by this beauty and to forget about shape and form. Your aim must be to combine these two aspects to create a successful piece.

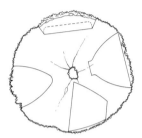

Fig 96 Log marked showing how to create different effects for decorative bowls

A burr-topped bowl in box elder

Decorative burr woods can be used to stunning effect in simply shaped vessels as shown below in burr oak

Rippled olive ash vessels from quarter-sawn wood

Rippled and quilted

This type of figure does not often penetrate deep into a log, and when it does, it usually finishes up in the veneer or musical instrument trade, where it will attract very high prices. If you are lucky enough to obtain such timber, it can be very attractive and makes wonderful bowls.

Burrs

Burred wood is among the most sought after of materials. If it is bought in log form, you can cut it and use it in a variety of ways, from bowls of formal purity through to

Spalt and decay

The presence of spalt and decay within a piece of wood can lead to the production of some dramatic pieces, they also often afford challenges to the technical skills of the turner.

Other figure and cuts

I have purposely avoided mentioning some grain formations that rely on the way in which the timber is cut – crotch and quarter-sawn, for example – because I feel that this figure is best used in flat objects. Many turners will, I am sure, feel that this proviso applies also to ripple and quilt. I have avoided bird's-eye and mazur on the grounds of cost and increasing rarity.

Wet wood

Turning wooden bowls 'wet' has been going on for centuries – most such coarsely made bowls were utilitarian. The majority of bowl-turners have rough-turned bowls to hasten drying (see the Salad Bowl, page 89), and I myself turn hundreds this way each year and then finish-turn them when they are dry. In Britain in the late 1970s a new trend was pioneered by Jim Partridge and Richard Raffan. Ultra-thin, delicate bowls were produced from 'wet wood' – that is, wood that still contains sap. A tree cut yesterday can be turned today, and this method of working removes at a stroke the seasoning problems most of us encounter. It's not quite as easy as it sounds, however – you have to work fast. If you are using small logs, you must use them before they split and start to dry out.

When these thin, delicate, almost porcelain-like bowls came on the market they drew a number of ceramic collectors to turned wood for the first time. Among the timbers that are suitable for this kind of work are holly, hornbeam, beech, sycamore, chestnut and the fruit woods. Although most of these are quite bland in colour, they work extremely well. Because the wood is wet, it cuts easily and offers little resistance to your tools. You can use high speeds, too. For example, a holly bowl with a diameter of 6in (150mm) can be turned at 2000rpm; if it were dry, a speed of 1200–1300rpm would be more appropriate. These bowls need to be turned very thin – $\frac{1}{16}$–$\frac{3}{16}$in (2–5mm) –

and very fast if the shape is not to be distorted. A bowl with a diameter of 6in (150mm) and 3in (75mm) deep should be thought of as an exercise that will take 20 minutes if you are to have any real chance of success.

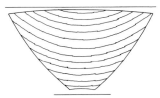

Fig 97 Wet-turned bowl with the centre core of the heart at the top edge; it is normal for the shrinkage to occur away from this as shown

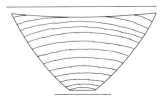

Fig 98 Wet-turned bowl showing the opposite reaction, with the core at the base. An ovalling effect will have taken place in each case when viewed from above

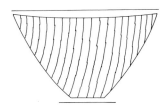

Fig 99 A wet-turned bowl, quarter-sawn, will have less distortion, but will also be less interesting

Bear in mind that the ability to work quickly and to recognize where to cut your bowl blanks from within a log, in order to ensure the stress release distortion factor is as equal as possible, are of great importance in minimizing wastage. Even turners who are competent in these skills often have a 10–20 per cent wastage because of unacceptable distortion. Do not be surprised if your early attempts in this field result in a 50–60 per cent wastage rate. Although this may sound dramatically wasteful, such a rate is not uncommon. Remember, too, that you will be using woods that should not cost you very much.

You will need to practise using the gouge, so that handling it effectively becomes second nature to you. When you can use the gouge fluidly and skilfully you will find you can turn two to three bowls from wet wood for every one you make from dry.

SMALL LOG BOWLS

SUGGESTED LATHE TOOLS

Pin chuck
Spigot, contracting or screw chuck
$\frac{1}{2}$in (12mm) or $\frac{3}{8}$in (9mm) bowl gouge
$\frac{1}{2}$in (12mm) Key modified spindle gouge
1in (25mm) or 1$\frac{1}{2}$in (38mm) French curve scraper
1in (25mm) or 1$\frac{1}{4}$in (31mm) curved-ended scraper

Log division

The photograph on page 110 illustrates three possible ways in which a small cherry log, 7–8in (175–200mm) in diameter, can be cut to provide different size bowls and to produce very different effects. Cutting the log in half will produce the largest bowls, and these will be flat topped. However, although they will be the largest, they will be the least attractive. The log centre pith core is boxed out, and the heartwood is at the top of the bowl, while the greater part of the shape is dominated by sapwood. Sapwood does not have the richness of colour that the heartwood has and often has a murky look, as is the case here.

A more attractive alternative, which still produces flat-topped bowls, is to cut the log so that the heartwood is in the base. The photograph shows how a log can be divided to give four bowls. Wood for two and three bowls can be produced in the same way, making for larger bowls showing the same characteristics. This approach gives more attractive results: most of the sapwood is removed, and, as the growth ring pattern emanates from the base, the wood has a strong, almost stacked veneer, elliptical effect.

The most dramatic visual effect, and the most challenging to make, is to cut the log into sections to make natural topped bowls. The photograph shows a log divided

to yield three such bowls, but two larger or four smaller bowls could also have been cut by dividing the wood differently. When these bowls are looked into, the shape appears to be elliptical, although this is an optical illusion, caused by the way the growth rings become stretched through the bowl's curvature. I sometimes true an unattractive log top into a more formally true form on a pneumatic drum sander.

The natural topped bowl phenomenon has produced some of the most unattractive, even downright ugly, bowls ever made. They are always a challenge, and the mistake people make is to try to make them before they have developed their basic turning skills sufficiently. Done well, however, they can be very attractive and dramatic.

Preparation

As a challenge, the instructions here are for making a small natural topped bowl from a dry cherry log. The one used as an illustration is 175mm (7in) in diameter and cut in such a way to yield three bowls. A section 6in (150mm) long was cut and divided into three, boxing out the pith core, and then cut into three segments vertically on the band saw. A flat section was cut on the base of each section, then a plywood disc, 5$\frac{3}{4}$in (146mm) in diameter, fixed with a nail through the centre, centrally on top of the curved log section. Wedges support the bowl section segments to allow safe cutting of the bowl blank into a disc. The plywood disc is used to cut a true circle, then the template disc is removed, and the nail hole gives you an automatic centre to drill a 25mm (1in) hole, some 2in (50mm) deep. This is drilled on the pillar drill, ready for chucking on an expanding or fixed pin chuck.

Chucking

The bowl blank was mounted on the Axminster chuck with the 1in (25mm) expanding pin jaws fitted.

Shaping the outside

A speed of 1300–1500rpm should be selected for a bowl of this size. Using a $\frac{1}{2}$in (12mm) bowl gouge, with the wings ground back, shape 90 per cent of the outside, in the same way as described in other bowl projects. There is a difference here though: cut only from the base to the lowest point of the log's curved top. You then cut back from the top to this curve, blending the surfaces together. If you do not use this method you run the risk of break-out at the top or, if the bark is still adhering, you may force it off.

You must now consider chucking to hollow the interior. If you are confident that your tool skills are good, try holding it in a spigot chuck – I use the $1\frac{1}{2}$in (38mm) O'Donnell jaws. If you have any doubts about your ability, go for a glue block, on which you can cut a dovetail tenon to grip in a contracting jaw chuck or drill a hole in the centre for a screw chuck. You will need a flat surface to bond on. The quickest bonding is to glue the block with gap-filling cyano-acrylate glue. Put glue on the waste block and accelerator on the bowl base and rub them very slightly together. This will bond in seconds and be ready to turn almost instantly.

Outside tooling

With your bowl re-mounted in or on your chosen chuck, refine most of the outside bowl shape. Leave the foot area a little heavier at this stage to provide support when you are hollowing the interior. Take light finishing cuts with the $\frac{1}{2}$in (12mm) Key modified spindle gouge as described in the instructions for the Salad Bowl (see page 90) or use your preferred method.

Internal hollowing

Hollowing can now begin with a bowl gouge, either a $\frac{1}{2}$in (12mm) or $\frac{3}{8}$in (9mm). The drill hole in the middle makes hollowing quite easy. Make fluid cuts that progressively open and deepen the centre, aiming for a constant wall thickness of around $\frac{1}{8}$in (3mm). With practice, you should be able to achieve this straight from the gouge, but if you do not have sufficient skill yet, you may need to use a scraper to remove ripples and to blend surfaces. If you need to do this, the methods described here should help you.

The problem most often encountered is getting a good blend between the intermittent cutting of the irregular edge and the continuous surface just below the shaped rim. Blend this area true with a French curve scraper to a constant wall thickness of $\frac{1}{8}$in (3mm). At this stage, leave the lower section of the bowl with a wall thickness of around $3\frac{3}{8}$–$\frac{1}{2}$in (9–12mm), which will damp down flex and vibration.

When you have successfully achieved a ripple-free blend of surface, proceed to tool the bowl thinner with the gouge, following this, if necessary, with a curved scraper to remove any ripples and undulations.

Do not try to use a scraper on the bowl anywhere near the top once it is very thin. The chances of a catch blowing it apart are very high. Great care must be taken at all times when using a scraper on thin work – and it must be sharp.

Refining the outside bowl with a $\frac{1}{2}$in (12mm) wings ground back bowl gouge

Sanding

You need to be careful when sanding items that do not have a continuous surface. There are three major pitfalls:

- If you hand-sand, any carelessness can result in bruised fingers. Point your fingers down and take care.
- Polish with a paper towel instead of cloth, especially on burrs, which can grab and do great damage to both you and your bowl.
- Take care that you do not abrade the edge to an uneven thickness.

I power-sand most of this type of bowl with the 2in (50mm) Velcro-backed discs and pads, working through the grits from 120 down to 400. Final abrading is with ultra-fine Scotch-Brite pads.

Shaping the bowl top on a pneumatic drum power sander

Finishing

This is a matter of personal choice, but as this is a decorative piece I usually apply a thin coat of pre-cat satin lacquer, which is left to dry for 15–18 hours before being cut back with very fine abrasive and ultra-fine Scotch-Brite pads. I then apply wax and polish to a satin lustre.

Final tooling

The footed base of your bowl is still larger than necessary, and it is now time to reduce it. It does not really matter which way you have chucked it, but the final shaping and

surface blending are best carried out with the 12mm (½in) Key modified spindle gouge. Sand and finish as previously described, then part off from the waste block or remove from the chuck.

Reverse-chucking

A concave recess must be created in the foot, and for this the bowl is reverse-chucked on to a wooden mandrel that is faced with foam rubber or carpet. This material should compress so that it is compatible with the inner curve of the bowl. The tailstock with a revolving centre is brought up and centred true in the base. This is tightened sufficiently to friction-hold the bowl to allow for the tooling of the foot. The small core that remains is removed with a sharp carving tool and sanded smooth.

You should now have a reasonably attractive small bowl from a small log that would most likely have been burned.

The finished dimensions of the bowl illustrated are 5½in (140mm) in diameter and 75mm (3in) high. Two more similar bowls were made from the other sections of log, which is not a bad return from a log section 7in (175mm) in diameter, cut 6in (150mm) long.

Bird's-eye maple bowl

Completed cherry bowl

A richly coloured and patterned bowl made in cocobolo

VESSELS

Vessel blank cut from a piece of rippled white ash and with shaping both inside and out almost complete

I feel there should be constant, steady evolution in woodturning. The developments may be very subtle, with slight changes being made to objects that we may have produced for years, but the goal is to perfect each one. On the other hand, each woodturner should seek new directions and challenges to develop and extend skills. In recent years I have been increasingly drawn to the vessel form. I regard as a vessel a container that is normally taller than its diameter, and made from end-grain timber. Some forms are quite rounded while others are elongated. Both open and enclosed vessels can be made, with the latter providing the greater challenge. Remember that the smaller the opening and the rounder the shape, the greater the challenge.

TALL VESSEL

SUGGESTED LATHE TOOLS

Contracting jaw chuck or small faceplate
¾in (18mm) roughing gouge
¾in (18mm) skew or square-ended chisel
½in (12mm) Key spindle gouge (modified)
1in (25mm) or 1½in (38mm) Key French curve scraper

Preparation

As an introduction to this kind of turning, this section shows the making of a moderately difficult piece.

The vessel illustrated was made from a piece of rippled white ash, 7½ x 4¾ x 4¾in (190 x 120 x120mm), cut from a fine log. The finished piece measured 7 x 4½ x 4½in (178 x 115 x 115mm).

The square should be mounted between centres and turned into a cylinder using a ¾in (18mm) roughing gouge. The speed for making throughout was 1000–1300rpm. The ends can be trued either with the point of a skew chisel, a spindle gouge or a parting tool. A parallel tenon/spigot, 2½in (64mm) in diameter and ¼in (6mm) long, was cut to go in my Axminster four-jaw chuck, which has a set of 2½in (64mm) contracting jaws. These jaws have a little dogtooth that bites into and grips the wood wonderfully. I use these jaws for gripping work up to 9in (230mm) long, but if you do not have this type of chuck or jaws, I suggest you use a small 3in (75mm) faceplate. You will need to add another ¾in (18mm) to the square in length. I suggest you use four screws that penetrate by ¾–1in (18–25mm) into the end grain for secure holding.

Shaping the outside

With the cylinder in the chuck or secured to a faceplate, you can begin shaping. Most of the outline form can be created with the ¾in (18mm) roughing gouge. To refine the shape you can use a ¾in (18mm) skew or square-ended chisel or the ½in (12mm) Key modified spindle gouge. At this stage you are aiming to create just over three-quarters of the finished shape before hollowing the interior. The bottom quarter is left purposely heavier at this stage to provide support while the hollowing takes place.

Hollowing the interior

The method is the same as for hollowing the boxes, but there is more to remove and you need to go much deeper. First, bore a hole down the centre, either with a drill or with the ½in (12mm) Key modified spindle gouge, supported by the tool rest, as explained in the box section (see page 95). The gouge is brought back to the top of the hole. The flute of the gouge face, which should be towards you, is tilted at an angle of 45 degrees out of the vertical. Remove the interior with a continuous series of pivoting, scooping cuts, deepening and opening up the centre as required and

Shaping the cylinder with a ½in (12mm) spindle gouge

Hollowing the interior with a ½in (12mm) Key spindle gouge

removing 95 to 98 per cent of the material in this way.

Hook or ring tools can be used instead. They are used in exactly the same way – that is, presented at an angle of 45 degrees out of the vertical.

Finally, true the surface with a 1in (25mm) or a 1½in (38mm) Key French curve scraper, depending on the size of vessel.

You could excavate the whole of the interior with a scraper, but this would be a slow method, and is usually resorted to only when the turner has not taken the time to learn how to use all the tools correctly. The scraper should be used for 2 to 5 per cent of the work.

Sanding

I usually hand-sand vessels of this type at this stage, even though the final shaping near the base of the outside has still to be completed. This is because the extra support is needed if the sanding process is to be successful. Sand the inside and all of the outside that is tool finished with flexible, cloth-backed, aluminium oxide abrasive paper. Work through the grits from 120 down to 400, before finishing with ultra-fine Scotch-Brite pads.

I have fairly small hands and can sand inside quite small openings. If your hands are quite large, you will find it easier to use foam-rubber-faced pressure sticks, which can be used to hold the abrasive to sand the interior.

Final shaping

After sanding to the stage outlined, final shaping of the outside is completed with a gouge and chisel. This is then blend-sanded as previously described.

Finishing

The vessel illustrated was finished with a thin coat of pre-cat satin lacquer applied with a mop brush. It was left to dry for 15–18 hours then cut back with 400 grit abrasive dipped in wax (to stop lacquer melt and drag). This was followed with an ultra-fine Scotch-Brite pad and wax. Once there was no sign of lacquer rings or build-up, polishing with a soft cloth produced the required satin lustre. A lathe speed of around 1200rpm was used for this process.

Parting off

With a narrow parting tool in one hand and supporting the vessel in the other, carefully part in a short way at the base. Do not cut so deep that the vessel starts to run out of true, or it could whip and hit the tool rest. Cut through the remaining material with a saw.

Completing the base

The base now needs completing, and there are several possibilities, including disc-sanding and using a Velcro-backed pad and disc in the pillar drill. However, I believe that every element of an article should be completed to the same standard. I used a 'dough-nut' ring chuck, which makes it possible to tool and sand the base to completion.

Dough-nut ring chuck

A dough-nut ring chuck is a home-made tool based on an idea by Jack Straka and further developed by Todd Hoya, both from the USA. It is made from two discs of finest Finnish birch plywood, ¾in (18mm), one solid, and one with a suitably sized, turned and tapered hole in the middle. Three small leather protection pads are glued in this. The solid disc is mounted on a faceplate ring. Three accurate, equally spaced holes are drilled near the edge of this and the hollow ring, all in alignment. Three equal lengths of ⅜in (9mm) threaded drill rod are secured with nuts and washers, one each side of the solid disc. These are adjusted to accommodate different sizes of bowl or vessel.

The vessel is inverted and the top is centralized against the solid plywood disc, with the hollow ring removed. This is now fitted over the three threaded rods. The base of the vessel should now protrude through the hollow ring. The washers and nuts are tightened to secure the ring supporting the vessel.

Do not allow the rod to protrude above the hollow ring more than is absolutely necessary because this could be very dangerous when you are tooling the base. This may all sound quite complicated, but once you have the system in place, it works well and enables you to tool the base of any in-curved bowl or tall vessel to perfection.

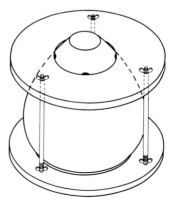

Fig 100 Dough-nut chuck

A selection of different size vessels made in rippled white ash

GALLERY

Spalted beech enclosed vessel

Burr buck eye bowl

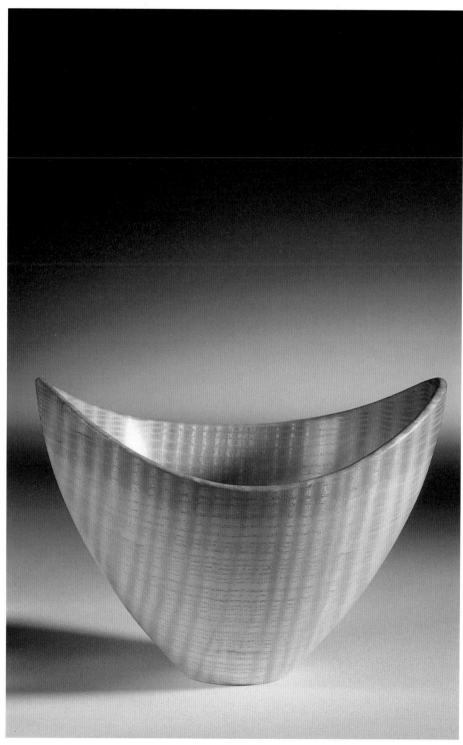

Shaped top rippled white ash bowl

Mountain mahogany box with spalted sapwood plus chatter work in the lid

Two burr buck eye bowls from the same block of wood – the smaller one coned from the larger one

Footed burr buck eye bowl

FURTHER READING:

Key, Ray	*The Woodturner's Workbook*, B T Batsford 1992
Marsh, Bert	*Bert Marsh: Woodturner*, GMC Publications 1995
Pain, Frank	*The Practical Woodturner*, Evans Brothers 1957
Pye, David	*Nature and Art of Workmanship*, The Herbert Press 1995
Raffan, Richard	*Turning Wood*, Taunton Press 1985
Regester, Dave	*Woodturning Step by Step*, B T Batsford 1993
Rowley, Keith	*Woodturning: a Foundation Course*, CMC Publications 1990

LIST OF SUPPLIERS:

Axminster Power Tools
Chard Street
Axminster
Devon, EX13 5DZ
Tel: 01297 33656
(lathes, chucks and tools plus 'Key' tools)

Frank Boddy's
The Woodworkers Superstore
Riverside Sawmills
Boroughbridge
North Yorks, YO5 9LI
Tel: 01423 322370
(all requirements plus wood)

Craft Supplies Ltd
The Mill
Millers Dale
Nr Buxton
Derbyshire, SK17 8SN
Tel: 01298 871636
(all requirements plus wood)

CSM Just Abrasives
95-96 Lewes Road
Brighton
Sussex, BN1 6WA
Tel: 01273 60093
(abrasives)

Fiddes
Florence Works
Brindley Road
Cardiff
South Glamorgan
CF1 7TX
Tel:01222 340323)
(all finishing materials)

Alan Holtham
The Old Stores
Wistaston Road
Willaston
Nantwich
Cheshire, CW5 6QJ
Tel: 01270 67010
(all requirements plus wood)

Multi Co Ltd
Paragon House
Flex Meadows
The pinnacles, Harlow
Essex, CM19 5TJ
Tel: 01279 444212
(graduate lathes and chucks)

Racal Health and Safety Ltd
Beresford Avenue
Wembley
Middlesex, HA0 1QJ
Tel: 0181 902 8887
(respirator helmets)

Rolston Timber
Hop Cottage
Worcester Road
Leight Sinton
Malvern
Worcs, WR13 5EQ
Tel: 01886 833612
(timber)

Stebcraft
PO Box 601
Bradford
West Yorks, BD9 6UU
Tel: 01274 496120
(drive centres)

Henry Taylor Tools Ltd
The Forge
Peacock Estate
Livesey Street
Sheffield, S6 2BL
Tel: 0114 234 0282
(manufacturer of turning tools including the 'Key' range)

USA
Craft Supplies USA
1287 East 1120 South
Provo
UT 84601
Tel: 1-800-551-8876
Tel: 801-373-0917
(all requirements plus wood, Taylor 'Key' tools & videos)

CANADA
Oneway Manufacturing
241 Monteith Avenue
Stratford
Ontario
N5A 2PG
Tel: 1-800-565-7288
(lathes and chucks)

NEW ZEALAND
Kelton Industries
Box 589
Kaitaia
Tel/fax: 0-9-408-5862
(Kel McNaughton centre saver)

INDEX